CHRISTIANITY
TRANSFORMED THE
WORLD

SHARON JAMES

TRUTHFORLIFE®

CHRISTIAN
FOCUS

Copyright © Sharon James 2021

paperback ISBN 978-1-5271-0647-5
epub ISBN 978-1-5271-0712-0
mobi ISBN 978-1-5271-0713-7

10 9 8 7 6 5 4 3 2

Published in 2021 and reprinted in 2022
by Christian Focus Publications,
Geanies House, Fearn, Tain, Ross-shire,
IV20 1TW, Scotland, U.K.
www.christianfocus.com
with
Truth For Life
P.O. Box 398000
Cleveland, Ohio 44139
truthforlife.org

Cover design by Pete Barnsley

Printed in the U.S.A.

CONTENTS

Dedicated with love and gratitude to

Edward
Bill
Peter
Nathanael and Benaiah

'One generation shall commend your works to another,
and shall declare your mighty acts.'
Psalm 145:4

In the secular West the labours of Christians down through the ages are often undervalued, and even demeaned, while there are wildly optimistic – and inaccurate – claims made for the roles played by atheists and the like. Sharon James' book helps to restore some equilibrium, and will be an encouragement to believers and a challenge to unbelievers. Of necessity, it is selective in dealing with issues like freedom, justice, life, the dignity of women, philanthropy, healthcare, education, work, and history, but it remains effective. That Marxism was responsible for the deaths of over 110 million people in seventy years is a fact worth knowing! Readers of Sharon James' work will learn much more, to warn and to inspire.

PETER BARNES

Lecturer in Church History, Christ College, Sydney, Australia
Minister of Revesby Presbyterian Church, Revesby,
New South Wales, Australia

The apostle Paul, writing to the very heart of the all-conquering, powerful Roman empire, says 'I am not ashamed of the gospel' (Rom. 1.16). The Lord Jesus Christ taught openly (Mark 14:48-49) and told His followers to be shining lights in the world and rubbed in, preserving salt. But too many Christians and Churches today feel like what they believe is out of date and barbaric; must be watered down, kept as some ugly little secret and have lost faith that it stacks up in our progressive, sophisticated age. In this brilliant book, Sharon James reclaims the ground and shows that nothing has done more for education, health, justice, the sanctity of life and dignity of women than this great Faith. A must-read 'for such as time as this'.

Headteacher, Fulham Boys School, London

I would commend this book to young people studying A level history as well as Christian teachers. It would also be a helpful read for anyone who wants to find out how the Bible, Christians and Christianity have impacted our world for the good. You will be greatly encouraged.

NAOMI OLIVER

Emmaus School, Trowbridge, UK

The real joy of Sharon James' book, *How Christianity Transformed the World,* is how she has been able to combine insightful stories and a breadth of engagement with personalities from history interwoven into a careful, perceptive and important theological narrative. This makes for an engaging read and leaves you wanting more, which is always a sign of a good book. One of the really attractive approaches in her book is how she manages to interweave the well-known personalities – William Wilberforce, Josephine Butler, Lord Shaftesbury – with less well-known names – Fidelia Fisk, Thomas Jones, Sarah Martin. This keeps the reader's interest as you discover new facts and I was in awe of the breadth of names brought to our attention.

The book is a work of theology and deeply important for that. The biblical foundations in the creation narratives, the linking of the liberties of Magna Carta to their biblical foundation and the recognition that our healthcare and education originated with Christianity are just some examples of how Christianity transformed the world. A reminder also that God calls us to minister and disciple in the world rather than to separate ourselves from it.

RICHARD TURNBULL
Director, Centre for Enterprise, Markets and Ethics, Oxford

Whether you're a believer or unbeliever in Christianity, this book will make you glad and grateful that you live in a world so profoundly and pervasively shaped by Christianity. And if you've been influenced to believe that the Christian gospel is a virulent intellectual infection that should be eradicated, that it robs people of joy and freedom, that it oppresses women and makes its heavenly-minded adherents of little earthly good, then you very much need to read this book. As Sharon James's extensive research reveals, real history tells a very different story—one that will fill you with all the right kinds of wonder.

JON BLOOM
Co-founder and Teacher, Desiring God

Christianity is good news to the world, despite critics' charges that it is oppressive and outmoded. Sharon James skilfully marshals Scripture, church history, and cultural analysis to set the record straight, showing the revolutionary impact of Jesus Christ on humanity. Buy five copies and give them to friends who are confronting today's secular bias.

JOHN FOLMAR
Senior Pastor, United Christian Church of Dubai

Acknowledgements

This book had its genesis when I was invited to give four talks at Word Alive 2019, with the title *How Christianity Changed the World*.[1] My thanks to the organisers of that event. Thanks also to those who attended the talks, those who asked great questions and contributed to the discussions, and those who asked me to put the talks into a book. I'm grateful to the Social Issues Team at Affinity, who subsequently published extracts from those talks in a series of articles.[2]

I work as part of a team at The Christian Institute. It's been a privilege to offer a variety of seminars to the team, and I always value their discussions and input. I am especially grateful for help given by Dave Greatorex and Toby Lucas. Of course, the views expressed in this book are my own, as are any and all mistakes made.

1   https://wordaliveevent.org/media/src/series/583/title/how-christianity-changed-the-world (accessed 17 November, 2020).

2   The talks were then summarised in a series of articles for the Affinity Social Issues Bulletin, 2020.

I am grateful to The Baroness Cox of Queensbury for providing the Foreword. I have been inspired by her faithful efforts to 'be a voice for the voiceless' over many years, and am thankful for the work of The Humanitarian Aid Relief Trust (HART).

My husband Bill has provided generous and unfailing support for all my writing projects over thirty-five wonderful years of marriage.

My late father, Erroll Hulse, had unshakeable and joyful confidence in the good purposes of God in history. His conviction that God is, and will be, glorified in all things, has shaped and informed all my thinking and all my writing.

Sharon James
London, 2020

Foreword

Nearly forty years ago, quite unexpectedly, I was given the opportunity of serving in British politics. At that time, I resolved to use this privileged position in order to be 'a voice for the voiceless', and since then, I have visited many different countries, including Sudan, South Sudan, Nigeria, Nagorno-Karabakh and Burma. I have witnessed the suffering of many who endure terrible oppression, discrimination, abuse – even modern-day slavery. But I, and my colleagues in the Humanitarian Aid Relief Trust (HART), hear often from our partners on the front lines of faith and freedom in troubled areas of the world. They are challenging injustice and abuse, and caring for the needy, often at great risk to themselves.

How is this possible? Quite simply, it is because of the fundamental biblical conviction that *all* human beings are to be respected because we are *all* created in the image of God.

Today it is often claimed that Christianity is a repressive and toxic influence. I have seen for myself that the evidence demonstrates otherwise. I have been told by partners in Burma that the Burmese government dislikes Christianity because it fosters genuine democracy, by encouraging individuals to think for themselves. What a wonderful tribute to the Christian faith and its underpinning of individual freedom and dignity! And so, I am delighted to commend this survey of how so many Christians through history have also sought to bring freedom and justice to their fellow human beings.

Sharon James is honest about the undoubted failures of some sections of the Church in the past, and she fully accepts that Christians do not have a monopoly of compassion. God has endowed all people with a conscience and with capacity to show love and mercy. But her account provides an engaging corrective to the jaundiced view of Christianity presented by so many today, including by many in our education system. Far from being a toxic and repressive influence in history, Christianity has in many ways transformed the world for the better. The biblical teaching that every human being is made in the image of God has been the foundation for our regard for human dignity and freedom. I witnessed the horrors of modern-day slavery during the war which raged in Sudan from 1989 to 2005 when, together with Christian Solidarity International, I had the poignant privilege of helping to rescue many hundreds of women and children from slavery. I appreciated with new fervour the extraordinary efforts of those such as William Wilberforce who tirelessly campaigned for legislation to abolish the slave trade in the British Empire. As we look back over the past two thousand years, and across the world, we find that many Christians have lived out Christ's self-giving love, often at great personal cost.

This book provides a clear and engaging overview of the positive impact Christians have had on society over the centuries, including sections on education, philanthropy and healthcare. I believe it also provides a challenge. The urgent needs of so many in the world today call out for a new generation of those who are willing to pray, to give, and to work to obey Christ's command to love God and to love our neighbour.

The Baroness Cox of Queensbury
Founder and CEO of HART
(Humanitarian Aid Relief Trust, https://www.hart-uk.org/)

Introduction

Many people today would agree that Christianity *has* transformed the world – but for the worse. The 'new atheists' don't just see Christianity as wrong, but evil. They believe that we need to be liberated from outdated ideas of moral absolutes. Science (not religion) can solve our problems.

The way history is sometimes presented is that Enlightened Rome (pagan) collapsed; then came the Dark Ages (religious superstition); but during the Renaissance and Enlightenment, human reason triumphed over religion. Humanity then entered the uplands of scientific progress unhindered by faith. Human virtue (without God) could achieve human rights, freedom and prosperity.

That simple narrative has been discredited.[1] Tom Holland,

---

1   David Bentley Hart, *Atheist Delusions: The Christian Revolution and Its Fashionable Enemies* (Yale University Press, 2010); V. Mangalwadi, *The Book that Made your World: How the Bible Created the Soul of Western Civilisation* (Thomas Nelson, 2011); R. Stark, *The Victory of Reason* (Random House, 2006).

author of *Dominion: The Making of the Western Mind*,[2] testifies that in his youth:

> I was more than ready to accept their interpretation of history: that the triumph of Christianity had ushered in an 'age of superstition and credulity', and that modernity was founded on the dusting down of long-forgotten classical values.

But reflection on the evidence changed his mind:

> The longer I spent immersed in the study of classical antiquity, the more alien and unsettling I came to find it. The values of Leonidas, whose people had practised a peculiarly murderous form of eugenics ... were nothing that I recognised as my own; nor were those of Caesar, who was reported to have killed a million Gauls and enslaved a million more. It was not just the extremes of callousness that I came to find shocking, but the lack of a sense that the poor or the weak might have any intrinsic value.[3]

Tom Holland set out to trace the impact of Christianity on Western civilisation, and discovered that the self-giving example of Christ, and the ethic of respect for all human life as made in God's image, are the *real* foundation of all those values we cherish.

---

2   Tom Holland, *Dominion: The Making of the Western Mind* (Little, Brown, 2019). The American release, is entitled: *Dominion: How the Christian Revolution Remade the World*.

3   Tom Holland, 'Why I was Wrong about Christianity', *The New Statesman*, 14 September 2016, https://www.newstatesman.com/politics/religion/2016/09/tom-holland-why-i-was-wrong-about-christianity (accessed 26 March 2020).

Introduction

Sociologist Rodney Stark has had a long and distinguished academic career, and written many books on the history of Christianity. For most of his career he made no particular religious profession. He argues:

> The success of the West, including the rise of science, rested entirely on religious foundations, and the people who brought it about were devout Christians.[4]

This is because Christianity teaches that God, the supremely rational being, has created mankind in His image. He has placed humans in an ordered and coherent world, with the task of stewarding and managing its resources, using their God-given gifts of reason and logic.

Another historian claims that Christianity has been:

> ... *the* most powerful agent in transforming society for the better across two thousand years ... No other religion, philosophy, teaching, nation, movement – whatever – has so changed the world for the better as Christianity has done.[5]

The purpose of this book is to pull together and summarise some of the findings of some of the longer works that have appeared recently. I give suggestions for further reading at the end of each chapter, and there is also a list of resources at the end. This book is not comprehensive, it's an introduction.

---

4   Rodney Stark, *Victory of Reason* (Random House, 2006), p. xi.

5   Paul L. Maier, *Foreword to Alvin J. Schmidt, How Christianity changed the World*, (Zondervan, 2004), p. 9. Paul L. Maier was former Russell H. Seibert Professor of Ancient History at Western Michigan University, and is now Professor Emeritus.

I want to provide a short and simple primer to help you to answer these common accusations:

- *Christianity is violent and intolerant*
- *Christians are on the wrong side of history*
- *Christianity is terrible for human rights*

Of course, this is a vast topic. Christianity today is the first truly global religion. A third of the world's people are nominally Christian. There is no way that the full impact of Christianity can be measured. And we need to remember that:

- *In the past, in the name of Christ, injustices have been wrongly perpetrated*
- *Institutional religion has to be distinguished from real living Christianity*
- *Christians don't have a monopoly on virtue and compassion*

But from the inception of the Christian Church at Pentecost, the followers of Jesus have sought to love their neighbour and to reflect God's moral character. We can trace at least some of the beneficial and widespread impact this has had. In chapters one and two we will consider the theme of freedom. Chapter three will look at the question of justice. We'll turn in chapters four and five to the protection of life and the dignity of women. In chapters six and seven we'll consider philanthropy and healthcare. Chapters eight and nine will deal with educational provision and the work ethic. In the final chapter we will contrast two views of history.

This overview gives a broad view of those through the centuries who have professed to be Christian. Mention of the positive achievements of a person or group does not imply validation or endorsement of their theology.[6]

You don't have to read the whole book consecutively. The chapters are self-contained, so you can dip in and out looking at the topics you find most interesting. To enable each chapter to be read alone, there is a small amount of overlap between some of them.

The consensus today in the media and the educational establishment is deeply hostile to biblical Christianity. Christians may respond by feeling defensive and afraid. But we don't have to be ashamed. Throughout history, Christ's true followers have done much good. This short, necessarily selective account is designed to present a positive response to the overly-negative story we often hear. I want readers to be confident that:

> A world from which the gospel had been banished would surely be one in which millions more of our fellows would go unfed, unnursed, unsheltered and uneducated.[7]

Let's begin to see how!

---

6   My 2017 Word Alive talks on the Reformation include material on the importance of truths such as the final authority of the Word of God, https://reformation-today.org/articles-of-interest/the-reformation-rediscovering-the-power-of-the-gospel-a-series-of-papers-by-dr-sharon-james-presented-at-the-word-alive-conference-2017-part-i/ (accessed 15 June, 2020).

7   Bentley Hart, p. 15.

1 Freedom

The Spirit of the Lord is upon me, because he has anointed me to proclaim good news to the poor. He has sent me to proclaim liberty to the captives and recovering of sight to the blind, to set at liberty those who are oppressed ... (Luke 4:18, ESV)

Joseph Kim was four years old when the great famine struck North Korea in 1994. Over a million North Koreans would die of starvation in the following years. Joseph's dad was one of them. His mother escaped to China, hoping to earn money to send back to her family. Joseph never saw her again. Aged sixteen, with nothing to lose, he risked his life by crossing the border to China.[1]

---

1   *The Guardian*, 18 October, 2015, https://www.theguardian.com/world/2015/oct/18/christianity-defectors-escape-route-north-korea (accessed 3 April, 2020); Joseph Kim, TED talk 2013, https://www.ted.com/talks/joseph_kim_the_family_i_lost_in_north_korea_and_the_family_i_gained/transcript? (accessed 3 April, 2020).

As I write, in early 2020, North Korea is probably the least-free country on earth. The government exerts a totalitarian control by means of a network of concentration camps and wide-spread arrests. Those who attempt to escape over the border to China are often caught and sent back to these concentration camps, or to execution. If they do elude capture in China, they are often told: 'Look for the Cross!'

For even though Christians in China are themselves under severe pressure from the authorities, many take huge personal risks to help refugees from North Korea.[2] Joseph, who had never heard of Christianity, was helped by such believers. He eventually reached freedom in the United States.

Tu Airong, a Chinese Christian, was sentenced to twenty years' imprisonment for his role in helping North Korean refugees escape to Thailand.[3] He, and many other Christians, willingly run such risks because they believe that human beings made in God's image have dignity and should enjoy freedom.

Many people assume that the liberty and justice that we take for granted today are the results of secular thinking.

In reality, the liberties and rights that we value in free societies are to a great degree based on the biblical conviction that all humans, made in God's image, are equal in dignity (Gen. 1:26-7).[4]

---

2   Timothy S. Shah, and Allen D. Hertzke (eds), *Christianity and Freedom*, Volume 2 (CUP, 2016), pp. 141-4.

3   Ibid., p. 143.

4   Larry Siedentop, *Inventing the Individual: The Origins of Western Liberalism* (Penguin, 2015); T. Holland, *Dominion: The Making of the Western Mind*, (Little, Brown, 2019).

In 2016, Cambridge University Press published a two-volume symposium, *Christianity and Freedom*, which incorporated years of research by a team of international scholars. The overall conclusion was that:

> ... free institutions hardly ever developed in places that were not influenced by Jewish and Christian ideas. Outside the Judeo-Christian tradition, it has been rare for thinkers to suppose that God endowed us with a nature of our own, that freedom is part of that nature ...[5]

The origin of the idea of 'human rights' is the concept of the person, which is founded on the biblical view that all people are created in the image of God. This is what affords equal dignity to every individual.[6] And the incarnation of Christ confirms the significance of our human condition. God taking human flesh underlines the dignity of the human person.

The historical reality is that regimes which have denied the existence of God, and followed an atheistic or 'hard secularist' political philosophy, have demonstrated the *least* regard for human rights. Where no God is acknowledged, the State can all too easily 'become God', with appalling consequences. R. J. Rummel spent years researching what he calls 'Death by Government'. *Democide*, (his word), is the intentional killing by governments of their own people. He concludes:

---

5   Shah and Hertzke, p. 29, quoting Remi Brague.

6   Edmund Matyjaszek, 'Human Rights: The Rise of the All Powerful State', pp. 229-52, in Lynda Rose (ed), *What are They Teaching the Children?* (VFJ/Wilberforce Publications, 2016).

Of all religions, secular and otherwise, that of Marxism has been by far the bloodiest ... [It] has meant bloody terrorism, deadly purges, lethal prison camps and murderous forced labor, fatal deportations, man-made famines, extrajudicial executions and fraudulent show trials, outright mass murder and genocide. In total, Marxist regimes murdered nearly 110 million people from 1917 to 1987. For perspective on this incredible toll, note that all domestic and foreign wars during the 20th century killed around 35 million. That is, when Marxists control states, Marxism is more deadly than all the wars of the 20th century, including World Wars I and II, and the Korean and Vietnam Wars.

There is a supremely important lesson for human life and welfare to be learned from this horrendous sacrifice to one ideology: No one can be trusted with unlimited power ... As a government's power is more unrestrained, as its power reaches into all corners of culture and society, the more likely it is to kill its own citizens.[7]

Militant atheism treats religion as an anti-revolutionary social force which must be suppressed by political measures. Under Communist governments, religion is regarded as a 'false consciousness' which should be eliminated through propaganda and re-education, or by force.[8]

---

7   R. J. Rummel, 'The Killing Machine that is Marxism', *The Schwarz Report*, 15 December, 2004, https://www.schwarzreport.org/resources/essays/the-killing-machine-that-is-marxism (accessed 8 April, 2020).

8   Nick Spencer, *Atheists: The Origin of the Species* (Bloomsbury, 2014), p. 234.

Response to Slavery

Slavery is the ultimate denial of human liberty, and

> ... of all the world's religions, including the three great
> monotheisms, only in Christianity did the idea develop that
> slavery was sinful and must be abolished ... slavery was once
> nearly universal to all societies able to afford it ... only in the
> West did significant moral opposition ever arise and lead to
> abolition.[9]

The Christian conviction that every human being is made in the image of God stood in stark contrast to the culture of the ancient world, which rested on brutal slavery.

The great Greek philosopher **Aristotle (384-322 BC)** taught that without slaves to do labour, enlightened people wouldn't have the energy and leisure to pursue wisdom and virtue. It never occurred to Aristotle that a slave might have the right to pursue wisdom and virtue! The philosopher **Plato (c. 428-c. 348 BC)** believed that slaves had no souls, so they had no human rights. Masters could treat them as they wanted. There was no concept of universal human dignity in ancient culture.

Of the approximately seventy million people in the Roman Empire, at any one time around a seventh of them, ten million, might have been slaves. It was socially acceptable for male freemen to use women, young men, children, and slaves for their own sexual gratification.

---

9   Rodney Stark, *For the Glory of God: How Monotheism Led to Reformations, Science, Witch-Hunts, and the End of Slavery* (Princeton University Press, 2004), p. 291.

Sheer violence, institutional and personal, was integral to ancient sexual culture.[10]

In this context the apostolic witness that 'in Christ we are all one, whether slave or free' (Gal. 3:28) was revolutionary. There were no pagan cults where slaves and free could both belong on an equal footing. For churches to admit free people and slaves as fellow members was unprecedented.

Early in the fourth century, **Lactantius (c. 250-325)**[11] in his *Divine Institutes* said that in God's eyes there were no slaves. **Chrysostom (c. 347-407)**, also in the fourth century, proclaimed that when Christ came He annulled slavery. He told the wealthy in his congregation to buy slaves, teach them a trade, and then set them free.

The Cappadocian **Father Gregory of Nyssa (335-395 AD)**, attacked slavery for its sheer arrogance and 'violation of the free nature of human beings made in God's image'. 'Do you condemn man to slavery whose nature is free and autonomous?' Gregory demanded.

> How much does rationality cost? How many obols [Greek coins] for the image of God? ... For He who knew human nature said that the entire cosmos was not worthy to be exchanged for the soul of a man.[12]

---

10 Kyle Harper, in Timothy S. Shah and Allen D. Hertzke (eds.) *Christianity and Freedom*, Volume 1, (CUP, 2016) p.134.

11 The abbreviation 'c.' stands for the latin word *circa*, indicating that the dates given are approximations.

12 Ibid., pp.133-4.

It took time to root out slavery in the Western world. But treating slaves with dignity as Christian brothers and sisters, embracing them in the Church family and giving them communion, all laid the way for arguing that as slaves were part of the body of Christ they should be freed. Over the centuries, increasing numbers of manumissions took place, and also increasing numbers of marriages between slaves and free. One such marriage took place when **Clovis II King of the Franks (r. 639-657)**[13] married his slave Bathilda in 649. She eventually mounted a campaign to halt the slave trade and redeem those in slavery. The **Emperor Charlemagne (r. 800-814)** also opposed slavery. By the eleventh century the last vestiges of slavery in Christendom were abolished.

The transatlantic slave trade brought back the horror on a wider and more terrible scale. When **Queen Elizabeth I (r. 1558-1603)** was told of the early efforts to take slaves from Africa to the Americas, she was outraged, and warned that the slave trade would call down the vengeance of heaven. But commercial interests prevailed. Between the reign of Elizabeth I and the end of the eighteenth century, about ten million African slaves were taken over to forced labour in the Americas (and they were the ones who didn't perish on the journey). Shockingly, by the eighteenth century, the prevailing legal and public opinion in England was that slavery was acceptable. Many people believed that the wealth and power of Britain would collapse without the slave trade.

---

13   The abbreviation 'r.' stands for 'reigned'.

Then, as now, people argued that if something was legal, it was acceptable. The evangelist **John Wesley (1703-1791)** disagreed, demanding:

> Can Human Law turn light into darkness or evil into good? Notwithstanding 10,000 laws, right is right and wrong is wrong still![14]

Wesley cheered on and encouraged **William Wilberforce (1759-1833)**, the best-known campaigner against slavery. Wilberforce became a Member of Parliament at the age of twenty-one, and was close friends with the young **William Pitt (1759-1806)**, Britain's youngest ever Prime Minister. Converted to Evangelical Christianity, partly through the influence of John Newton, Wilberforce was 'moved by his religion to do a great thing for humanity' and found that cause in the abolition of slavery.[15] On his deathbed Wesley wrote to Wilberforce:

> Unless God has raised you up for this very thing you will be worn out with the opposition of men and devils, but if God is for you, who can be against you?[16]

Wilberforce often had need of that encouragement! On 12 May 1789, he rose to his feet in the House of Commons and delivered an eloquent, passionate, closely researched

---

14 John Wesley, *Thoughts Upon Slavery*, London 1774, p. 34, https://docsouth.unc.edu/church/wesley/wesley.html (accessed 23 December, 2019).

15 Melvyn Bragg, *12 Books that Changed the World* (Hodder and Stoughton, 2006), p. 160.

16 Quoted in John Pollock, *Wilberforce* (Lion, 1977), p. 105.

speech that lasted four hours.[17] The response? 'We need more evidence!' That delaying tactic would be used again and again over the next eighteen years. Year after year, Wilberforce introduced a bill to outlaw the slave trade. Year after year the establishment prevaricated.

He was vilified as a national traitor by many. English military hero Lord Nelson spoke of 'the damnable Wilberforce and his hypocritical allies'.[18] Sometimes he nearly achieved success. In 1796 his bill was thrown out by seventy-four votes to seventy. Just four votes short. The bill fell because about a dozen MPs who had promised support had not bothered to show up: they'd gone off to the opera, or into the country.

Eventually in 1807 the bill to abolish the slave trade passed by a staggering 283 in favour and sixteen against. Wilberforce wept as the crowded House of Commons gave him a standing ovation. Twenty-six years after that, just before his death, on July 26 1833, Wilberforce received word that Parliament passed the abolition act, freeing 700,000 slaves.

The abolition of slavery was not Wilberforce's single-handed achievement, but it was his single-mindedness that 'saw the campaign through'. His legacy extended beyond the abolition of slavery – it 'was the foundation of the worldwide human rights movement'.[19] Wilberforce:

---

17   William Wilberforce, 'On the Abolition of the Slave Trade', Speech in Parliament 12 May 1789, immediately published in several versions.

18   Bragg, p. 170.

19   Ibid., p. 173.

... personified the Christian arm of the Enlightenment at its best and ... set the world on a different and a finer course ...[20]

He was the leader among countless faithful campaigners. One of those often forgotten was **Zachary Macaulay (1768-1838)**. Macaulay was the behind-the-scenes researcher, a statistician who tirelessly worked eighteen-hour days to provide the hard facts.[21] During his long fight against injustice he was vilified, slandered and attacked, but he persevered.

Another forgotten hero was the evangelical **Granville Sharp (1735-1813)**. As a young man he was moved by an encounter with a young runaway slave in London docklands. He single-mindedly devoted his life to the cause of abolition. In 1772, he argued that English law stretching back to Magna Carta did not justify the practice. He later memorably remarked that 'no power on earth' can make slavery right. In the famous Somerset case, Sharp applied for a writ of *habeas corpus* for the freedom of James Somerset, arguing that as he was not the property of his master he could not be forcibly shipped to Jamaica. After the Somerset case, English courts consistently upheld the rights of former slaves against their masters.

The popular stereotype of Western Christian missionaries is that they imposed their culture on others, and laid the way for exploitation and removal of freedom and justice.[22] In

---

20 Ibid., p. 175.

21 Faith Cook, *Zachary Macaulay* (Evangelical Press, 2012).

22 Individual missionaries may have been guilty of cultural insensitivity. But missionaries were at the forefront in spreading education, printing, literacy, reform, the dignity of women, and political

reality, many Evangelical missionaries were at the forefront of the campaign to abolish slavery. In 1823, when thousands of slaves rebelled in Guyana (then called Demerara), the planters crushed the revolt. They blamed **John Smith (1790-1824)**, an evangelical missionary, and sentenced him to death. He died due to harsh conditions in prison.[23]

Missionaries who had been expelled from British slave colonies because of their opposition to slavery toured Great Britain making fiery speeches and distributing petitions. They could describe, first-hand, the horrors they had seen. As a result, more than ninety-five per cent of adult Wesleyan Methodists signed petitions against slavery. After the British government finally abolished slavery in 1833, missionaries continued to campaign against bad treatment of ex-slaves. One can draw a contrast with those European countries ruled by secular enlightenment governments. In France, for example, intellectuals spoke against slavery, but they didn't have the numbers of evangelical converts in the population who they could mobilise to agitate against slavery.[24]

In America, slavery continued for a further thirty years. It is shameful that so many Christians defended slavery. But many

---

democracy. *Christianity and Freedom*, Volume 1, pp. 367-86. During the nineteenth century evolutionary theory resulted in academic studies of different races and cultures that were deeply racist. By contrast, missionaries working in the field often recognised cultural diversity and pioneered its study and preservation.

23 *Christianity and Freedom*, Volume 1, p. 380; 'John Smith, Martyr-Teacher to the Slaves of Demerara', https://missiology.org.uk/blog/john-smith-demerara/ (accessed 28 April, 2020).

24 *Christianity and Freedom*, Volume 1, p. 384.

others heroically resisted it. Thousands of runaway slaves were led to freedom in the North and in Canada by both black and white abolitionists, who organised a network of secret routes and hiding places that came to be known as the Underground Railroad. One of the heroines of the Underground Railroad was **Harriet Tubman (1822-1913)**, a former slave who on numerous trips to the South helped hundreds of slaves escape to freedom. Finally, in 1863 **Abraham Lincoln (1809-1865)** ended slavery in America by issuing the 1863 Emancipation Proclamation.

The story of slavery in America is deeply disturbing. One Christian slave reported that his master served him communion in the morning, and then whipped him in the afternoon for arriving a few minutes late to his shift. Meeting in clandestine prayer meetings out of work hours could be punished by brutal flogging. The other side however is that there are countless inspiring stories of courage and sacrifice. The dignity and spiritual power of the Christian testimony of those suffering dreadful abuse was later analysed by **Martin Luther King (1929-1968)** who developed a whole theology of suffering from the experience of black believers suffering discrimination. Famously, he wrote:

> We are caught in an inescapable network of mutuality, tied in a single garment of destiny.[25]

---

25 Martin Luther King Jr, *Letter from a Birmingham Jail*, 1963, paragraph 4, https://www.africa.upenn.edu/Articles_Gen/Letter_Birmingham.html (accessed 23 December, 2019).

We are all descended from the same first parents, we are all made in the image of God, we all have equal value, and we all have a real responsibility for each other.

It is often forgotten that the slave trade was not the monopoly of Europeans. From the eighth century, the Islamic slave trade flourished. Muslim slave traders captured millions of Africans, and sold them as slaves in Arabia, Mesopotamia, the Ottoman Empire and North Africa.[26] Few today remember that over a million white Europeans were kidnapped and sold into slavery, forced to endure barbaric conditions. The palace of the Sultan of Morocco was built entirely with Christian slave labour.[27]

Over in North America, a definitive study of the indigenous North West coastal Indian tribes showed that up to a third of the population was made up of slaves, and that masters could kill slaves if they chose.[28]

Today there are more slaves in the world than ever before. The International Labour Organisation claims that there are 20.9 million victims of human trafficking worldwide. Many Christians are in the front line of opposing slavery and people trafficking. The International Justice Mission is a significant,

---

26 Sheldon M. Stern, 'The Atlantic Slave Trade: the full Story', *Academic Questions*, Summer 2005, p. 17, https://eric.ed.gov/?id=EJ844790 (accessed 28 April, 2020).

27 Giles Milton, *White Gold: The Extraordinary Story of Thomas Pellow and Islam's One Million European Slaves* (John Murray, 2005); Stark, *For the Glory of God*, pp. 301-4.

28 Stark, pp. 293-5, citing Leland Donald, *Aboriginal Slavery on the Northwest Coast of North America* (Berkeley, CA: UC Press, 1997).

international Christian network fighting abuse, but there are others.

The global curse of people trafficking is partly fuelled by the exploitation of women and children in the 'sex trade', which is promoted and worsened by the sexual revolution and its demand for unlimited sexual 'freedom'. Those trapped in slavery pay the highest price. Worldwide there are countless Christians devoted to rescuing and rehabilitating the victims of this trade.[29] Christians oppose pornography, and oppose the buying and selling of sex, which are major factors behind the vast increase in trafficking.

Christianity – The Source of Our Liberty

A famous debate took place in 1550 in the Spanish city of Valladolid, on whether or not the Indians in Spain's empire in the 'New World' had the right to self-government. Bishop and social campaigner, Bartolomé de las Casas, argued that pagan or not, every human being had been made equally by God and endowed with the same spark of reason:

> All the peoples of the world are humans, and there is only one definition of all humans and of each one, that is that they are rational.[30]

He was making the point that every human being created by God has rights that derive from God.

---

29 Dignity Freedom Network, the International Justice Mission, and Stop the Traffik, among many other organisations.

30 Tom Holland, *Dominion: The Making of the Western Mind* (Little, Brown, 2019), p. 331.

Still in our day, around the world, there are Christians who are willing to risk their freedom and even their lives to uphold that principle. People like those humble Chinese Christians who take such risks in order to help refugees like Joseph Kim.

All true followers of Christ are called upon to do the same.

Further Reading

Timothy S. Shah, 'Christianity and Freedom: Ancient Roots and Historical Innovations', in Timothy S. Shah and Allen D. Hertzke, *Christianity and Freedom*, vol. 1 (CUP, 2016), pp. 1-29.

M. Brockway and Allen D. Hertzke, 'Transnational Christian Networks for Human Dignity', in Timothy S. Shah and Allen D. Hertzke, *Christianity and Freedom*, vol. 2 (CUP, 2016), pp. 133-60.

R. J. Rummel, 'The Killing Machine that is Marxism', *The Schwarz Report*, 15 December, 2004, https://www.schwarzreport.org/resources/essays/the-killing-machine-that-is-marxism (accessed 8 April, 2020).

Rodney Stark, *For the Glory of God: How Monotheism Led to Reformations, Science, Witch-Hunts, and the End of Slavery* (Princeton University Press, 2004), pp. 291-365.

2 Religious Liberty

Dirk Willems had been thrown into prison in Asperen, the Netherlands, and was awaiting execution. His crime? He had been baptised as a Christian believer, and he had hosted illicit religious meetings in his home. Early in 1569 he managed to knot rags into a rope, and escape from a prison window. Fleeing for his life, he made it safely across a frozen dyke.

The jailer who was pursuing him, a heavier man, fell through the ice. Hearing his desperate cries for help, Dirk turned back to pull him out of the water.[1] He was re-captured, and later burned slowly at the stake.[2]

---

1   Image of this event: https://i2.wp.com/mennoworld.org/wp-content/uploads/2014/04/dirkwillems20icon-437x580.jpg?fit=1024%2C1024 (accessed 28 April, 2020).

2   Thielman J. van Braght, *The Bloody Theatre or Martyrs Mirror of the Defenceless Christians who baptized only upon confession of faith, and who suffered and died for the testimony of Jesus, their Saviour, from the time of Christ to the year A.D. 1660*, 1660, http://www.homecomers.org/mirror/dirk-willems.htm (accessed 7 April, 2020).

One of the most common accusations levelled at Christians is the claim that Christianity has a shameful record of intolerance and persecution. How should we respond?

That encounter on the frozen dyke shows that in the name of Christ, acts of violent persecution have wrongly been perpetrated. Dirk was a victim of religious intolerance.[3] But his own act of grace to his persecutor showed that he was a true disciple of the Lord Jesus Christ.

> When they hurled their insults at him [Jesus Christ], he did not retaliate; when he suffered, he made no threats. Instead, he entrusted himself to him who judges justly. (1 Pet. 2:23)

Sadly, Christians have not always followed Christ's example as consistently as Dirk Willems did. But we will see in this chapter that the biblical world view provides the most secure foundation of the rights of the individual, including the right to religious freedom.

The Biblical Basis for Religious Liberty

Jesus taught that we are to:

> Give back to Caesar what is Caesar's and to God what is God's. (Mark 12:17)

Caesar (*aka* the State) does not have the right to demand everything from you. You were not made in the image of Caesar. You were made in the image of the One who made Caesar. Caesar has no right to tell you what to believe. God,

---

3   Gelderland in The Netherlands was at that time under the rule of Catholic Spain.

your Creator, alone has authority over your soul. God calls citizens to obey civil authorities (Rom. 13:1-8; 1 Pet. 2:13-14), but obedience is not to be unlimited. When there is a clash of demands, we obey God rather than men (Acts 5:29). We can infer from this that governments should not coerce the consciences of their citizens. The apostle Peter exhorted believers to *honour* the Emperor – and *fear* God (1 Pet. 2:17).

The basis for respecting religious freedom goes back to creation. Men and women are made in God's image. They are rational beings, given the capacity to worship, love and relate. Genuine worship, love and relationship cannot be coerced. God calls His people to '*choose* the good' (Deut. 30:19). The Old Testament contains numerous condemnations of external religious ritual, performed without the free and willing love of the heart. God promised the good of the land to those who *willingly* obey Him (Isa. 1:19-20).

Luke Goodrich, an American lawyer, argues:

> ... religious freedom is a basic issue of biblical justice, rooted in the nature of God and the nature of man ... human beings are created for relationship with God, and God desires relationship with us. But a relationship with God can never be coerced. It must be entered into freely ... The definition of a violation of religious freedom: when a government uses its coercive power to interfere in the relationship between God and man. When the government does that, it's violating the created order, and perpetrating an injustice.[4]

---

4   Luke Goodrich, *Free to Believe: The Battle over Religious Liberty in America* (Multnomah, 2019), p. 21.

The Early Church

Building on this biblical foundation, several of the early church fathers argued that religious freedom is an individual natural right possessed by all people, regardless of religious convictions. The phrase 'religious liberty' was used for the first time in history in Tertullian's *Apology*, written c. 197 AD. **Tertullian (c. 155-220 AD)** warned magistrates:

> See to it that you do not end up fostering irreligion by taking away freedom of religion and forbid free choice with respect to divine matters, so that I am not allowed to worship what I wish, but am forced to worship what I do not wish. Not even a human being would like to be honoured unwillingly.[5]

He went on to argue that religion consists of more than rituals, it has to come from inner conviction. Superficial observance makes a mockery of genuine piety. Persecution will never result in genuine devotion. Ten years later, when Christians were undergoing persecution in Carthage, North Africa, Tertullian wrote a letter to the Roman Governor in which he argued:

> It is a fundamental human right, a privilege of nature, that every man should worship according to his own convictions: one man's religion neither harms nor helps another man. It

---

5   Quoted in Robert L. Wilken, *Liberty in the Things of God: The Christian Origins of Religious Freedom* (Yale University Press, 2019), p. 11.

is assuredly no part of religion to compel religion – to which free-will and not force should lead us.[6]

When the **Emperor Constantine (r. 306-337)**[7] issued the Edict of Milan in 313 AD, this did not 'impose' Christianity on the Empire (that would, regrettably, come later). The Edict of Milan allowed Christianity to operate freely. The Edict has been called the 'World's first universal declaration of religious freedom'. Christians, and all others, were to have the free and unrestricted right to follow that mode of religion which to each of them appeared best.

The North African theologian **Lactantius (c. 250-325)** proposed a policy of religious freedom to the Emperor Constantine, a policy demanded by both justice and piety:

> ... the butcher's trade and piety are two very different things ... if you want to defend religion by bloodshed, torture and evil, then at once it will not be so defended, it will be polluted and outraged. There is nothing that is so much a matter of willingness as religion ...[8]

Lactantius taught that humans made in God's image are endowed with a conscience, and he defended the right of each individual to follow their conscience. He was adamant

---

6   Quoted in Timothy S. Shah, and Allen D. Hertzke (eds.), *Christianity and Freedom: Volume I Historical Perspectives* (CUP, 2016) p. 8.

7   Constantine ruled firstly the Western Empire; and then the whole Empire from 324.

8   Lactantius, *Divine Institutes*, V. 19, 23, quoted in *Christianity and Freedom*, Volume 1, pp. 9-10.

that laws may punish offences, but they cannot change the conscience.

Disastrously, within about ten years, Constantine's policy had become more coercive. Over time 'the Church was transformed from a voluntary association into a public institution,'[9] and 'obedience to Caesar and obedience to God began to merge'.[10] By the fifth century some Christian theologians such as Augustine were arguing for coercion against the Donatists and others deemed to be heretics.[11] But in subsequent years, the early foundational thinking in favour of freedom of conscience did re-appear.

Alcuin: True Faith Cannot Be Forced

Alcuin (c. 735-804) was one of the leading educationalists of the eighth century. Born in Northumbria, he transformed the curriculum at the cathedral school in York. He was then invited by the Emperor Charlemagne to join his court in Aachen in 782. Alcuin taught Charlemagne himself, as well as the Emperor's sons and daughters. He was internationally recognised as one of the most brilliant men of the age. He tried to persuade the Emperor not to impose Christian ways on the Saxons. He wrote:

> Faith arises from the will, not from compulsion. You can persuade a man to believe, but you cannot force him. You

---

9   Wilken, p. 26.

10   Ibid., p. 34.

11   In the first instance, the use of force against the Donatists was justified because some of them had turned to violence. Wilken, p. 31.

may even be able to force him to be baptised, but this will not instil the faith within him.[12]

The 'Sacral' Era: Religious Liberty Undermined

This biblical principle was undermined, and all too often forgotten, during the 'sacral' era. This was the period of history when it was assumed that a territory had to have a single faith. It was thought that there would be disorder and fragmentation if that unity were undermined. The terrible outcome of that was the persecution of dissenters. *The Pilgrim Church*[13] is an account of dissent through those centuries during which religious unity was enforced. It gives a vivid picture of believers' churches, or gathered churches, which were all too often vilified as heretical and violently persecuted. Today, Christians would unequivocally agree that such persecution was wrong, and not a real reflection of true Christianity. We understand (and concede) that the accusations of atrocities sometimes thrown against Christianity may be genuine criticism of the intolerance which was the inevitable result of 'sacral' thinking.[14]

---

12 *Christianity and Freedom*, vol. 1, p. 68.

13 Edmund. H. Broadbent, *The Pilgrim Church* (Lulu Press, Reprint 2018).

14 Although we should, equally, be aware that there has often been exaggeration and distortion in descriptions of both the Inquisition and the Crusades. See Rodney Stark, *Bearing False Witness: Debunking Centuries of Anti-Catholic History* (Templeton Press, 2016); and Rodney Stark, *God's Battalions: The Case for the Crusades* (HarperOne, 2009).

By the sixteenth century, that 'sacral principle', (that Church and State were coterminous), had obscured the biblical truth of religious freedom. During the Reformation, the mainstream or magisterial reformers such as Luther and Calvin recovered the biblical truth about salvation. But they maintained the principle that everyone in a territory should belong to the same church, and bitterly opposed those who believed that Scripture demanded gathered churches of professing believers. The magisterial reformers stood *with* the Roman Catholics in enforcing the death penalty on those who believed that baptism should follow profession of faith, rather than be administered to all infants born within a certain territory.

Religious Liberty Recovered

The so-called 'Anabaptists', and then the Baptists, recovered the foundational biblical principle of liberty of religion. One leading Anabaptist was **Balthasar Hubmaier (c. 1480-1528)**. He wrote a powerful plea for religious freedom in 1524: *Concerning Heretics and those who burn them*. He accepted that magistrates have a duty to uphold law and order, but he denied their power to enforce religion. He wrote:

> Now it is obvious to everyone ... that the law which demands the burning of heretics is an invention of the devil.[15]

Similarly, **Claus Felbinger (d. 1560)**:[16]

---

15   William R. Estep, *The Anabaptist Story* (Eerdmans, 1975), p. 197.

16   The abbreviation 'd.' indicates the year of death.

God wants no compulsory service. On the contrary, He loves a free, willing heart that serves Him with a joyful soul and does what is right joyfully.[17]

The *Schleitheim Confession* (an Anabaptist confession of faith) was written in 1527. Written in the context where magistrates used torture and the death penalty to enforce religion, it acknowledged that God gives magistrates authority to punish evil and promote good (Rom. 13). But it *denied* that God gives magistrates authority to enforce religion.

It is often said that Anabaptists rejected *all* civil authority. Certainly, the *Schleitheim Confession* said that true believers should not serve as magistrates. But that is because in 1527 if you served as a magistrate you would necessarily be directly involved in enforcement of religious intolerance.[18] You would be expected to condemn your fellow believers to torture and death. It would be the equivalent of asking a Chinese Christian to join the Communist Party and help suppress religious dissent. To condemn all Anabaptists as opponents of civil authority fails to understand them in their historical context.

The first full defence of religious liberty in English was written in 1612 by the Baptist **Thomas Helwys (c. 1575-1616)**. His biblical treatise against religious persecution was called *The Mystery of Iniquity*. He had the audacity to send a personally inscribed copy to King James I, writing:

---

17   Estep, p. 197.

18   George H. Williams, *The Radical Reformation* (Westminster Press, 1962), pp. 184-5.

> If the King's people be obedient and true subjects, obeying all human laws made by the King, our Lord the King can require no more, for men's religion to God is betwixt God and themselves, the King shall not answer for it; neither may the King be judge between God and men.[19]

Helwys believed that forced faith is no faith at all. The king has no power to coerce the soul. Each individual answers to God alone in matters of religion. Helwys argued that freedom of conscience should be granted to all, including Catholics, Jews and Muslims. James I was not impressed. Helwys was imprisoned in Newgate, in horrible conditions, and died there in 1616.

The next landmark biblical defence of religious freedom came in 1644. *The Bloudy Tenent of Persecution for the Cause of Conscience Discussed*[20] was written by the Baptist **Roger Williams (1603-1683)**. In modern English it might be called 'The Bloodthirsty Principle of Persecution'. Roger Williams had come to strong Puritan convictions while studying at Cambridge University. In 1631 he sailed over to Massachusetts. He argued that force never produces genuine faith, that forced worship is abominable to God, and that people's consciences ought never to be violated or constrained. He maintained that the magistrate has no place in controlling the Church:

---

19 http://www.centerforbaptiststudies.org/resources/iniquity.htm (accessed 11 December, 2019).

20 R. Williams, *The Bloudy Tenent of Persecution for the Cause of Conscience Discussed*, 1644, https://oll.libertyfund.org/pages/1644-williams-bloody-tenet-of-persecution-letter (accessed 29 April, 2020).

That religion cannot be true which needs such instruments of violence to uphold it.[21]

He compared coercing conscience to spiritual rape.[22]

The Protectorate (1653-1659) offered a brief interlude of greater religious freedom in England. Oliver Cromwell believed that freedom of conscience should be extended not just to professed Christians, but also to Jews (and to any who were not a threat to the civil order).[23] But the Restoration of the Monarchy in 1660 ushered in an era of fierce persecution. The great Puritan **John Owen (1616-1683)** argued in *Truth and Innocence Vindicated* that thought and worship should be free. He criticised magistrates for invading God's prerogative to govern the souls of men. He drew on the writings of Tertullian and Lactantius, and argued that liberty of conscience is not based on the law of society, but on the law of nature. Liberty of conscience is a consequence of human freedom. 'Liberty is necessary unto human nature.'[24]

William Penn (1644-1718) was converted in 1659 at the age of fifteen. Aged twenty-two he converted to the Quaker movement, which meant that his family, for a while, disinherited him. He was imprisoned several times in the Tower of London due to his faith. Famously, in 1670, a judge

---

21 Mostyn Roberts, *The Subversive Puritan: Roger Williams and Freedom of Conscience* (Evangelical Press, 2019), p. 140.

22 Roberts, p. 133.

23 Which is why Roman Catholics were not included, they were thought to be a threat to the civil order as their first loyalty was to the authority of the Pope.

24 John Owen, quoted by Wilken, p. 164.

ordered a jury to find him guilty. The jury refused. The judge then fined and imprisoned the jury. This led to a famous test case. Twelve other judges found in favour of the jury, and ruled that juries should not be subject to intimidation.

William Penn founded the colony of Pennsylvania, and was famous for his fair and good relations with the Lenape North American Indians. He insisted that faith is the gift of God, so it cannot be forced, and that force may make hypocrites, but it can make no converts. He argued that denial of liberty of conscience is:

> ... an affront to God, for it invades the divine prerogative, and divests the Almighty of a Right due to none beside himself.[25]

John Locke (1632-1704) wrote his *Letters Concerning Toleration* between 1689 and 1692 in the aftermath of the European wars of religion. He argued that toleration is the chief characteristic mark of the true Church and that belief cannot be compelled by violence.[26]

At the roots of the Christian articulation of the importance of religious liberty are the following principles:

1. Religion is an inner conviction that cannot be coerced
2. Every human being is made in the image of God so should be afforded dignity
3. Each individual should be free to follow their religious conscience

---

25 William Penn, *The Great Case of Liberty of Conscience*, quoted in Wilken, p. 167.

26 Ibid., pp. 169-79.

4. God is only honoured when devotion and worship are willingly and freely given

At one time these were radical ideas. But today, whatever our genuine differences of conviction about either baptism, or the established Church, we would all agree on the need for freedom of conscience.

What About 'Proselytising'?

Many today suggest that to persuade people to change religion is 'abusive'. We should always condemn any effort to 'induce' professions of faith by means of material persuasion or coercion. Forced conversion or profession is wrong. But freedom *to* convert is a fundamental human freedom. Religious freedom has to include the freedom to change religion so long as conversion is free and voluntary. Vishal Mangalwadi, an Indian convert to Christianity, argues:

> A state that hinders conversion is uncivilised because it restricts the human quest for truth and reform.[27]

Mangalwadi illustrates this with a powerful account of the life of his friend **Dr Rochunga (Ro) Pudaite (1927-2015)**. Ro was born into the Hmar tribe in North East India, who were widely feared for their violence. Rochunga's parents lived in squalor and poverty. Brutality was the norm, and women and children were the main victims:

---

27 Vishal and Ruth Mangalwadi, *Carey, Christ and Cultural Transformation* (Authentic,1999), p. 67.

Evil spirits – real or imaginary – constantly harassed the Hmars. Demons were feared and worshipped because they brought disease. Medicine was unknown. Revered priests and witch doctors killed endless numbers of chickens, goats and pigs as sacrifices to appease the angry spirits. Ro believes that only exceptionally callous people would say that his tribe should have been left alone in its (imagined) 'pristine way of life'.[28]

Although the ruling British authorities had forbidden all efforts to reach this people, one brave Scotsman ignored that ruling in 1910. He walked for seven days over mountain trails to share the truth of Christ's offer of forgiveness and peace with God. That was the catalyst that eventually impelled Rochunga's father to send his little boy away to the nearest primary school, ninety miles away. He hoped that in time his son could translate the Bible into the Hmar language. Eventually, Rochunga not only translated the New Testament into Hmar, but went on to found eighty-five schools, a college, and a hospital. The culture was transformed. Mangalwadi writes:

> The Bible generates hope for all peoples. Ro thinks that it is no virtue to romanticize the miseries of a primitive tribe that lives at the mercy of natural elements, germs, demons, and unscrupulous, authoritarian priests. The Bible set his imagination free to dream what his tribe ought to be – educated; free to interact with neighbours and enemies;

---

28 Vishal Mangalwadi, *The Book that Made your World: How the Bible Created the Soul of Western Civilization* (Thomas Nelson, 2011), p. 358.

able to overcome hunger, hate, and disease; and ready to contribute to the world. Some advocates of 'multiculturalism' condemn people to live in the Stone Age.[29]

Some Western liberal academics suggest that cultures should be left alone, and that it is abusive for Christian missionaries to seek to share the Bible with them. That would have the effect of locking indigenous cultures in the past, and denying people the chance to hear the gospel. But those liberal academics would be outraged if they were told that their 'historic cultural heritage' is 'Christian', so they should maintain that identity and never change.

Is Religious Liberty Just a 'Private' Matter?

At the turn of the twentieth century a leading Dutch theologian and statesman, Abraham Kuyper, developed the concept of 'sphere sovereignty'.[30] This articulated the biblical truth that God has ordained various spheres of human activity. Most basic of all are the family and the Church. Leaders of these (usually fathers in the family and ministers or elders of the church) will be answerable to God at the last day for how they fulfil their trust. They should not overstep the mark and interfere with each other, for example, elders should not micromanage what goes on in church families. 'Intermediate' institutions, or spheres of authority, provide a buffer between

---

29 Mangalwadi, *The Book that Made your World*, p. 368.

30 James D. Bratt, *Abraham Kuyper: Modern Calvinist, Christian Democrat* (Eerdmans, 2013), pp. 130-48; 379-82; James McGoldrick, *Abraham Kuyper: God's Renaissance Man* (Evangelical Press, 2000), pp. 62-72; 158-66.

the individual and the State. In God's common (or everyday) grace they provide some protection against tyranny (where a State exercises absolute power over every individual). God has ordained government (Rom. 13) to restrain evil and promote the common good. Government leaders will answer to Him for how they fulfil that task. But the State should not interfere in the internal workings of other spheres, except in clear cases of law breaking (for instance, fraud or violent abuse).

The 'Naked Public Square'?

Many assume that if religion is kept out of the public square it will leave a neutral, tolerant space in which all can flourish. But emptying the public square of the Christian conviction that all humans are created in the image of God, with real dignity and freedom, makes space for a hard secularism which is far from neutral. It is based on a world view which sees Christianity as toxic and Christian morality as repressive. This world view dominates the major institutions of the West. It is deeply intolerant.[31] As R. J. Rummel has documented, anti-Christian regimes oversaw the murder of over a hundred million people in the last century.[32]

In our own day, we face fresh dangers, including the intolerance of identity politics. In *The Madness of Crowds*, Douglas Murray warns powerfully of the totalitarian dangers

---

31 Richard J. Neuhaus, *The Naked Public Square* (Eerdmans, 1984).

32 R. J. Rummel, 'The Killing Machine that is Marxism', *The Schwarz Report*, 15 December, 2004, https://www.schwarzreport.org/resources/essays/the-killing-machine-that-is-marxism (accessed 8 April, 2020).

of 'liberal overreach', where views which 'hurt the feelings' of 'victim minorities' are silenced.

If Christians run away from engagement in the public square and restrict their testimony to a privatised bubble of personal devotion and corporate worship, this leaves the way open for opponents of biblical Christianity to push back into the private sphere itself.

For example, some demand legislation against 'spiritual abuse'. But in a therapeutic culture, *any* preaching which calls sinners to repentance can be viewed as 'abusive'. For the State to be called on to legislate in this way would represent an overweening intrusion into Church life.

There are also threats to family privacy and freedom. Some claim that children from the youngest age must be taught about their 'rights' to sexual freedom or to choose their own 'gender identity', whatever the religious convictions of the parents. In the United Kingdom, parents are not allowed to withdraw their children from 'relationships education'.

The fundamental right to freedom of thought and speech is under threat as well. In 2018, a British doctor, David Mackereth who had worked for the NHS for nearly thirty years was dismissed from his role as a health and disabilities assessor at the Department for Work and Pensions. The reason? His conviction, on moral and scientific grounds, that sex is immutable. Chillingly, the tribunal panel that dealt with his case ruled that:

... belief in Genesis 1:27, lack of belief in transgenderism and conscientious objection to transgenderism in our judgment are incompatible with human dignity...[33]

This panel, on behalf of the State, claim the right to force a doctor to say things he does not believe to be scientifically or morally true. So Dr Mackereth has the 'religious liberty' to think what he likes in the privacy of his own head, but he is penalised for speaking what he believes.[34]

We need to be able to articulate the fundamental human right of religious liberty (which is based on biblical principles). Equally, we need to be alert to where that liberty is being eroded.

Persecution Today

A much harsher persecution is a daily reality for millions of people in the world. The places today where there is worst religious persecution are the nations where biblical Christianity has had the least impact. Of all the major faith groups, Christians suffer the most persecution. It was estimated that in 2020, 260 million Christians worldwide face high levels of persecution for their beliefs. In eleven countries there are 'extreme' levels of Christian persecution.[35]

---

33   Dr David Mackereth v The Department for Work and Pensions & Advanced Personnel Management Group (UK) Ltd [2019] ET 1304602/2018 at para. 197.

34   This concerning ruling is open to challenge.

35   *Open Doors*, https://www.opendoorsuk.org/persecution/ (accessed 27 March, 2020).

One country where Christians have come under severe pressure is China. The Christian Church there continues to grow despite opposition. Such extraordinary growth is probably unprecedented since the days of the early church. Between 1975 and 2010, the number of evangelicals exploded from 2.7 million to over 75 million.[36] At present there is ever increasing state pressure. In this context many Chinese Christian lawyers are courageously defending the freedoms not only of Christians but of others too, at risk to their own freedom and safety.[37]

Toleration or Freedom?

When the transcendent God is respected, we understand that each individual made in His image is answerable to their Creator for the state of their heart. So we don't just appeal for religious 'toleration'. That implies that it is a gift that can be given or withheld by the civil authorities.

Rather we insist that religious freedom, or liberty of conscience, is a natural right that belongs to all people made in the image of God. A biblical understanding of this principle is the only sure bulwark against totalitarianism: the overweening claims of an all-powerful state. That is why Christians today play a disproportionately large role in advancing religious freedom as a universal right:

> Because Christianity denies that the state is the ultimate arbiter of human life, it challenges all attempts – whether

---

36 *Operation World*, 7th Edition (Biblica Publishing, 2010), p. 216.
37 *Christianity and Freedom*, Volume 2, pp. 182-3.

Communist, theocratic, ethnic nationalist, or authoritarian – to impose a single authority in state and society ... Careful field research demonstrates the outsized role of Christian communities in defending religious freedom and human rights .... Pledging fealty to an authority higher than the state, Christians strive to carve spaces for autonomous civil society and conscience rights that underpin democratic governance.[38]

We should grieve that through the centuries there have been times when the institutional Church, in the name of Christ, has engaged in religious persecution and intolerance. This was an appalling perversion of biblical teaching. Today, Christian believers may hold differing convictions about baptism (or establishment), but we unite in giving thanks for the heroic testimony of Dirk Willems and all those who over the centuries have stood firm for the principle that faith must be free not forced. God's Word is the foundation for upholding religious liberty.

Further Reading

Robert L. Wilken, *Liberty in the Things of God: The Christian Origins of Religious Freedom* (Yale University Press, 2019).

---

38   Allen D. Hertzke, 'Introduction: Christianity and Freedom in the Contemporary World', in *Christianity and Freedom*, Volume 2 (CUP, 2016), pp. 4, 11.

3 Justice

Grace[1] lived with her husband John and five children in a rural area of Uganda. John worked as a butcher, Grace grew crops for sale on their small plot. When John fell ill and died, stronger members of his family tried to force Grace out of her home and off her land. Often a widow will find all the crops on her land destroyed in the night. Or the house will be knocked down around her and the children. Or it might even be burned down with them inside. An estimated ninety per cent of those living in rural Africa south of the Sahara have no proof of ownership for land where they live and work, leaving them vulnerable to violent land-grabbing.[2]

---

1   Names have been changed.
2   By 2020, 1.5 billion of the world's urban poor will live in informal settlements and slums without any secure right to their property. UN-HABITAT, 'Secure Land Rights for All.' Widows are particularly vulnerable to land theft. There are more than 115 million widows living in extreme poverty around the world, with half a billion children depending on these widows for survival. *The Guardian*, June

In Grace's case, she had, on paper, some legal protections. But police had been paid off by the violent thugs. Unless the widow can match the bribes she will never get justice. Grace refused to leave her home, but had to walk twenty-five miles to put her case to higher officials. They too wanted bribes. After several futile and wasted journeys, she was in despair.

Once the International Justice Mission found out about her case, the Ugandan lawyers on their team defended Grace and managed to secure her the documentation she needed to be able to stay in her home.[3]

The International Justice Mission was founded in the 1980s by Gary Haugen, an American lawyer who felt outraged that so many well-meaning attempts to help the poor were worse than useless when the poor were unable to secure justice. What's the point of giving a poor widow a loan to start up her own business, if as soon as she makes a profit, it is stolen from her and she can get no redress?

You will never get social and economic justice until you have legal justice, including property rights. A fundamental cause of poverty is the absence of the rule of law. If someone works hard, but their profits are stolen and there are no means of justice, that destroys all incentive.[4] When some government

---

23, 2011, https://www.theguardian.com/commentisfree/2011/jun/23/international-widows-day-support (accessed 28 April, 2020).

3   'Grace's story', International Justice Mission, https://www.ijm.org/our-work/land-theft (accessed 26 March, 2020).

4   Wayne Grudem and Barry Asmus, *The Poverty of Nations: A Sustainable Solution* (Crossway, 2013), pp. 114-15, 149-55, 160. If people are to be able to work and see the fruits of their labour, there must be laws against stealing and cheating others; there must also

officials and their friends are above the law, it means that what you work hard for can be requisitioned by the powerful, or stolen by those with the means to bribe higher officials.

The African editor of *The Economist* remembers a three-hundred-mile journey in Cameroon from Douala to Bertoua. He was in a large truck carrying 30,000 bottles of beer from a Guinness factory. The journey by road should have taken six hours. Four days later the truck arrived, having been stopped forty-seven times at road blocks. Only two thirds of the load was still in the truck. The rest had gone on bribes. At the thirty-first road block the driver dared to object. But the person stopping the truck simply asked: 'Do you have a gun?' 'No', said the driver. 'Well', the man at the road block replied, 'I have a gun, so I know the rules'.[5]

The fact that we instinctively feel outraged by such behaviour reflects God's gift to humanity of reason and conscience.

Wherever justice is upheld we should give thanks to God. Our triune God is characterised by perfect righteousness. He is the great lawgiver. The Creator has placed His moral law on the hearts and consciences of all the people He has created (Rom. 2:15). Each will have to give account to Him, including rulers.

---

be laws against fraud, the violation of contracts, and causing harm to others by selling defective and dangerous products. Laws must be fairly, effectively and swiftly enforced, and everyone in the nation must be subject to these laws.

5   Ibid., pp. 265-6.

Through history, rulers have been tempted to use power for their own advantage. In the Old Testament, God's prophet Elijah condemned King Ahab when he forcibly took Naboth's vineyard (1 Kings 21). God expects rulers to dispense justice fairly.

> Do not pervert justice; do not show partiality to the poor or favouritism to the great, but judge your neighbour fairly. (Lev. 19:15)

> Acquitting the guilty and condemning the innocent: the LORD detests them both. (Prov. 17:15)

> This is what the LORD says [to the King of Judah]: Do what is just and right. Rescue from the hand of the oppressor the one who has been robbed. Do no wrong or violence to the foreigner, the fatherless or the widow, and do not shed innocent blood in this place. (Jer. 22:3)

> Learn to do right; seek justice. Defend the oppressed. Take up the cause of the fatherless; plead the case of the widow. (Isa. 1:17)

The heart of God for justice is captured beautifully in the prophet Isaiah's poetic depiction of the coming Messiah:

> Behold, My Servant, whom I uphold;
> > My chosen one in whom My soul delights.
> > I have put My Spirit upon Him;
> > He will bring forth justice to the nations.
> He will not cry out or raise His voice,
> > Nor make His voice heard in the street.
> A bruised reed He will not break
> > And a dimly burning wick He will not extinguish;

> He will faithfully bring forth justice.
> He will not be disheartened or crushed
> > Until He has established justice in the earth;
> > And the coastlands will wait expectantly for His law.
> (Isa. 42:1-4, NASB)

Isaiah was writing in the context of the abysmal failure of God's servant Israel to maintain justice and righteousness. The national scandals of oppression and injustice offended the righteous God. So God would send His own Servant who would uphold justice where Israel failed. The Servant's mission was to establish God's own justice and righteousness. And the extent of the mission was universal, not only to the Jews, but to the 'distant coastlands'. In the Gospel of Matthew the prophecy is applied directly to the Lord Jesus (Matt. 12:18-21).

In the New Testament Paul taught that all rulers are God's 'servants' or 'deacons' placed in society to keep order by punishing evil and rewarding good (Rom. 13:1-8). Rulers, like all people, have God's moral law placed on their consciences. Each will answer to God at the Day of Judgement for how they have fulfilled their trust.

The Biblical Foundation for Magna Carta (1215)

The 800th anniversary of the signing of Magna Carta was celebrated in 2015. Over eight centuries this has symbolised the right of the people to limit the power of the government. In most of the anniversary celebrations, there was a dismal failure to realise that Magna Carta rested on biblical foundations.

In the centuries before Magna Carta was framed, Anglo-Saxon kings understood that their role, ideally at least, was to provide justice for their people. The underlying assumption was that God is ruler of the earth, the supreme lawgiver. God appoints kings to enforce justice. Any king who failed in that duty was no true king.

Alfred the Great ruled from **871 to 899**. He quoted extensively from the Bible in the introduction to his Code of Laws. He saw himself in the tradition of God-appointed kings who would be held accountable to God at the Last Day for how they ruled. His laws were based on the Bible, and the biblical concept that people should be treated justly:

> The recognition of the unique and inviolable status of the human person, as seen in the Bible, was the bedrock of all English law on the 'person'.[6]

In 973, **King Edgar (r 959-975)** pledged in his Coronation Oath to deliver justice, equity, and mercy. The coronation oath which established a covenant between ruler and people reflected the radical biblical truth that the one who rules should be like one who serves (Luke 22:26). The Ten Commandments provided a framework for Anglo-Saxon law.

This understanding of the king's responsibility before God to deliver justice continued after the Norman Conquest. In his Coronation Charter, **Henry I (r. 1100-1135)** vowed to be a 'good king' and abolish injustice, according to the godly model. But then came King John, who ruled from 1199-1216.

---

6   Edmund Matyjaszek, in Lynda Rose,(ed.), *What are they teaching the Children?* (VFJ/Wilberforce Publications, 2016), p. 233.

He ruled with gratuitous cruelty and injustice. He forced wealthy widows to marry the nobles who could offer him the largest bribes. He was widely believed to have murdered his own nephew, fifteen-year-old Arthur (a rival claimant to the throne). Those were just top of a long list of vice and violence. What could be done?

By this time, theologians had reflected deeply on how to react to tyranny. **John of Salisbury (c. 1120-1180)** was a churchman educated in Paris, who wrote the first comprehensive work of western political theory. He argued that a tyrant who despised the law – and with it the natural law and justice of God – was no ruler at all.[7]

One of those influenced by this teaching was **Stephen Langton (c. 1150-1228)**, an English theology professor teaching in Paris. Langton was responsible for the division of the biblical text into the chapters which we still use today, and he wrote commentaries on most of the books of the Bible. He dealt carefully with the God-given responsibilities of kings to rule justly. In his commentary on Deuteronomy he castigated kings who abuse their position to satisfy their own greed.

In 1207 Stephen Langton was appointed as Archbishop of Canterbury. Given his reputation as a fierce critic of those who abused power, King John refused, at first, to let him back in the country. Several years later however, back in England, Stephen Langton and others drew up the document we now

---

7   Thomas Andrew, *The Church and the Charter* (Theos, 2014), pp. 37-9, https://www.theosthinktank.co.uk/cmsfiles/archive/files/Reports/The%20Church%20and%20the%20Charter.pdf (accessed 28 April, 2020).

know as Magna Carta as a way of attempting to curb the king's tyrannical power.

Magna Carta began by affirming the rightful authority of the king. This reflected the biblical teaching that God appoints rulers to maintain civil order (Rom. 13:1-8; 1 Pet. 2:13-14). Just as important, Magna Carta made it clear that the king's authority was not unlimited. The king could not help himself to the property of his subjects; or make up laws to suit his own ends; or exploit the judicial system to enrich himself by collecting bribes.

In short, the charter established the principle that no one, not even the king, is above the law. This chart traces some of the ways that biblical principles influenced important sections of Magna Carta.[8]

Biblical Teaching	Magna Carta
God expects leaders in society to actively seek justice for the vulnerable and exploited (Isa. 1:17)	Introduction: King rules by grace of God
God appoints rulers to administer justice (Rom. 13:1-8; 1 Pet. 2: 13-14)	Clause 45: King to appoint competent and fair judges

---

8   https://www.bl.uk/magna-carta/articles/magna-carta-english-translation (accessed 28 April, 2020).

Kings will be held to account by God for whether they have kept His laws (I Kings 21; 2 Sam. 11-12)	Implied throughout: The King is not above the law; e.g. Clause 55: fines that the King had taken unlawfully to be returned; Clause 61: a group of elected barons to hold King to account if he broke the laws of the Charter
'Give to Caesar what is Caesar and to God what is God's' (Luke 20:25)	Clause 1: King cannot interfere arbitrarily in affairs of the Church; Clause 63: the Church shall be free
God expects judges to acquit the innocent and condemn the guilty (Prov. 17:15)	Causes 39 and 40: Jointly embody what have become the rights of *habeas corpus* (banning arbitrary detention and providing for trial by jury)
God condemns judges who take bribes or who favour the rich over the poor (Exod. 23:2-3,6-8; Deut. 16:18-20; Prov. 29:4)	Clause 40: Justice not to be sold, denied or delayed
No-one to be convicted without two or more witnesses (Deut. 19:15)	Clause 38: No-one to be convicted without testimony of credible witnesses

Proportionate justice (Exod. 21:23-5; Lev. 24: 17-22)	Clause 20: Proportionate justice
It is wrong to take away a person's means of making a living (Deut. 24:6)	Clause 20: People's means of livelihood not to be removed
One law for all, whether citizens or aliens (Lev. 24:22)	Clause 60: Points towards the equality of all before the law, a principle to be developed further in later centuries
Standard weights to be used in trade (Lev. 19:35-6)	Clause 35: the importance of justice in trade: standard measures to be used throughout the realm
Warning against kings exploiting their position to despoil people (1 Sam. 8:10-18)	Clauses 12 and 14: consent to be secured to taxes and other impositions to prevent arbitrary rule
Private property to be respected (Exod. 20:15; Deut. 19:14)	Clauses 12 and 14: Private property to be respected

Ever since Magna Carta was agreed in 1215, it has been used to protect life, liberty and property, and as the basis for constitutional rights and liberties around the world. That is something for which Christians can thank God. Certainly, at the time, the legal rights that Magna Carta spoke of, applied only to freemen. But it set the trajectory for these freedoms to be extended to everyone. Over the twists and turns of the centuries, with many reversals and advances, these ideas have come to dominate the legal landscape. The influence of Magna Carta spread to the USA and most countries in the West.

Baroness Caroline Cox has been at the forefront of humanitarian work in some of the most dangerous places on earth for many years. She believes:

> ... it is the Judeo-Christian tradition with its inherent respect for the human individual and its cherishing of the concept of individuals' rights and freedoms, which has generated and sustained the most humanising and humanitarian internationally recognised laws and policies, such as the abolition of slavery and the concept of Genocide.[9]

A research project of many years' duration by Robert D. Woodberry showed that where there has been the most impact of Bible-believing mission in the world, there are governments which are most respectful of human rights, and the rule of law, and least prone to tyranny.[10] It is a historic fact that individual freedom and rights are most prevalent where Christianity has had the greatest impact.

While engaged in open air work in a major university town in England, a graduate law student from China approached my friend. 'I'd like to find out more about Christianity,' she

---

9   Caroline Cox, 'Holding the Line', in Lynda Rose, (ed.) *What are they Teaching the Children?* (VFJ/Wilberforce Publications, 2016), p. 343.

10 R. D. Woodberry, 'Protestant Missionaries and the Centrality of Conversion Attempts for the Spread of Education, Printing, Colonial Reform, and Political Democracy', in *Christianity and Freedom*, Volume 1, pp. 367-90.

said. 'I don't understand why it is that only Christian judges refuse to take bribes.' We know why. God is a God of Justice. And He expects us to uphold justice too.

Further Reading

Wayne Grudem and Barry Asmus, *The Poverty of Nations: A Sustainable Solution* (Crossway, 2013), pp. 114-5, 134-5, 149-55, 223-43.

Vishal Mangalwadi, *The Book that Changed your World: How the Bible Created the Soul of Western Civilization* (Thomas Nelson, 2011), pp. 249-73.

Alvin J. Schmidt, *How Christianity Changed the World* (Zondervan, 2004), pp. 248-70.

4 Protecting Life

God the Giver of Life

In Spring 2018, Perumalla Pranay, a Christian from the 'Dalit' caste, married his childhood sweetheart, Amrutha in Andra Pradesh, India. This cross-caste marriage meant that Amrutha was rejected by her higher caste family. Six months later she and her husband were delighted to find that they were expecting a baby. But on the way out of a hospital appointment near their home, Perumalla was hacked to death by contract killers hired by his father-in-law. The pavement was stained with the blood of this young husband, who was so looking forward to the birth of his first child.

Perumalla was killed because the caste system views Dalits as of lesser worth, and as possessing no dignity. Some believe that the scale of injustice and abuse caused by the caste system makes it one of the single most serious human rights issues in history.[1] Today in India, it is Christians who are in the forefront of offering Dalits hope and dignity and the knowledge that they, along with all people, are made in the image of God.

Think back to the aftermath of the disobedience of our first parents. After the Fall, their first-born son Cain murdered his younger brother Abel. This was the first time a man had shed the blood of another man. God demanded: *'Where is your brother?'* Cain replied, *'Am I my brother's keeper?'* To which God responded:

> The voice of your brother's blood is crying *to me* from the ground (Gen. 4:10).

Perumalla Pranay's blood also called out to God. God will hold his killers, and the one who hired them, accountable. For God is the Creator and Giver of life. The followers of Christ know that we are indeed 'our brother's keeper', called to care for and defend fellow human beings.

Genesis 1:27 explains that human beings are distinct from the rest of creation. We bear the image of God. This wonderful truth:

> ... explains the purpose of redemption, culminating in the Cross. Why has God been so determined to rescue us, at such an immense cost? Would He have launched such an extravagant rescue mission for something insignificant or of trifling worth? No! God made man as the pinnacle of

---

1   Mark Woods, 'Telling a Better Story: How India's Christians are fighting for dignity for Dalits', All India Christian Council network, 4 September, 2018.

His creation. We have extrinsic dignity – derived from the intrinsic dignity of the One whose image we bear.[2]

After the flood, God told Noah:

> And from each human being, too, I will demand an accounting for the life of another human being.
>> 'Whoever sheds human blood,
>>> by humans shall their blood be shed;
>> for in the image of God
>>> has God made mankind ...' (Gen. 9:5-6).

God's moral law summarised in the Ten Commandments is a perfect expression of His moral character. The sixth commandment is 'You shall not murder' (Exod. 20:13). John Ling writes:

> Protection of human life is a recurring theme in Scripture. Uniquely in the created order it is only the lives of human beings that enjoy this special protection. The Sixth Commandment, 'You shall not murder' (Exod. 20:13), stands out as a great beacon to protect all innocent human life. 'Innocent' here does not mean those 'without sin', but those 'without harm'. Killing is permitted [in the Bible] in the cases of capital punishment, just wars and in self-defence, but killing of the innocent is strictly forbidden.[3]

When King David was brought to repent for his sin of murder, he confessed to God: 'Against you, you only have I sinned'. (Ps. 51:4). How could he say that? He had wronged Uriah. He

---

2   John. R. Ling, *When does Human Life Begin?* The Christian Institute, p. 8, alluding to R. C. Sproul.

3   Ibid., p. 14.

had wronged Bathsheba. He had wronged the baby who died. But it was God who had given life to Uriah, Bathsheba and her baby. David had despised God, the Giver of life.

Supremely Christians affirm the dignity of every human life because God Himself, in Christ, became flesh. Christ was incarnate, made flesh, from the moment of conception. If Jesus Christ took on human life as a single cell, our life also begins at conception.

God, the Giver of life, demands that human life made in His image should be protected from conception to natural death.

Sanctity of Life Defended in the Early Church

Turning to the historical record, Christianity spread rapidly during the first three centuries in the face of opposition and persecution. There were probably no more than a few thousand Christians in 40 AD. By the third century, Christianity was growing at the rate of forty per cent per decade. Sociologist Rodney Stark has calculated that by 350 AD there were more than thirty-three million Christians in the Roman Empire out of a total population of sixty million.[4] He argues that a significant factor in that extraordinary growth was the Christian ethic of defending the sanctity of life, which (contrary to today's feminist thinking) worked for the protection of women as well.

---

4   Rodney Stark, *The Rise of Christianity* (HarperCollins, 1997), p. 7.

Abortion was widely practised in Greco-Roman society. Leading philosophers justified the practice. Plato argued that it should be used as a means of population control.[5] As well as destroying the life of the child, it was very dangerous for the mother. Women were often forced into it by their masters (if they were slaves) or by their husbands.

Abortion was condemned by the early church and the church fathers, and by a series of church councils. This ethic of a respect for life saved countless unborn infants and their mothers. **Basil of Caesarea (330-379)** mobilised Christians to help women who were facing unwanted pregnancies. He also helped stage public protests against the activities of the guild of abortionists, who sold aborted infant bodies to the manufacturers of beauty creams. He was just one of many Christians trying to save the unborn.[6]

Many pagan philosophers approved of infanticide (the killing of newborns, or their abandonment and exposure). It was commonly practised in Greco-Roman society, particularly if infants were weak, sick, disabled or female.

In the year 1 BC, a travelling worker in Egypt, wrote to his wife at home. She was expecting a baby. He wrote:

> Many greetings. Know that we are still in Alexandria. Don't be anxious. As soon as I receive my wages I will send them up to you. If, may you have good luck, you should give birth, if

---

5   Plato, *Republic*, 5.461, translated F. M. Cornford (Oxford University Press, 1945), p. 161.

6   Alvin J. Schmidt, *How Christianity Changed the World* (Zondervan, 2004), p. 59. For more on Basil of Caesarea, see pp. 91, 130.

it is a boy keep it. If it is a girl, throw it out. I cannot forget you. I beg you not to be anxious.[7]

If it is a girl, throw it out! That reflected a widespread and nearly universally accepted practice.

The early Christians opposed this. They rescued and cared for infants whenever they could. Benignus of Dijon was a second-century Christian who lived in southern France. He rescued unwanted babies, those surviving failed abortions as well as abandoned infants. He then cared for and protected them. But for that reason he was killed.[8] Eventually, Christian influence prompted the **Emperor Valentinian (r. 364-375)** to outlaw infanticide and child abandonment in 374 AD.

It wasn't just infants who were regarded as expendable in the Roman Empire. Morally depraved emperors had no qualms about taking human life. **Emperor Tiberius (r. 14-37 AD)**, under whose reign Christ was crucified, loved to watch people being tortured. **Emperor Caligula (r. 37-41 AD)** on one occasion arbitrarily killed every one who served in his palace. He forced parents to witness the execution of their sons.[9]

As mentioned in chapter two, in 313 AD, Emperor Constantine issued the Edict of Milan, which for the first time gave Christianity legal status in the Roman Empire. Once Constantine was Emperor, he initiated social reforms

---

7   Jeremiah J. Johnstone, *Unimaginable: What Our World Would Be Like Without Christianity* (Bethany House, 2017), pp. 25-6.

8   Schmidt, p. 153.

9   Ibid., p. 57.

such as the abolition of crucifixion and the emancipation of slaves, as well as the discouragement of infanticide.[10]

The violence and cruelty of gladiatorial shows is still remembered. The Roman Empire at its height ruled 2.5 million square miles. Many subjected peoples were enslaved, and could be killed for the entertainment of citizens. The Colosseum in Rome, dedicated by **Emperor Titus (r. 79-81 AD)**, could seat 70,000 spectators. This huge venue, and others like it around the Empire, saw the deaths of many thousands of gladiators. The early Christians were sometimes condemned to death in the arena. Even during lulls in persecution they consistently spoke out against this barbarity. Such games were banned in the Eastern Roman Empire by the Christian Emperor Theodosius by the end of the fourth century.

The last gladiatorial conquest took place in Rome in 404, after a military victory over the Goths. Gladiators fought furiously. As each one was wounded, the audience would signal whether they should be killed or not. Especially privileged people could descend into the arena to get a closer view of the dying agonies of the victims. But on this occasion, someone else forced his way down into the arena. A Christian called Telemachus from Asia had been moved to the depths of his soul when he saw thousands flocking to view the slaughter. He had entered the event not to enjoy the spectacle but to witness against it.

'In the name of Christ, Stop!' he shouted, while attempting to separate two of the gladiators. The crowd was enraged at this

---

10   Diana Lynn Severance, *Feminine Threads* (Christian Focus, 2011), p. 66.

challenge to their entertainment. Telemachus died amid a hail of stones and other missiles. But his work was accomplished at the moment he was struck down. His death turned the hearts of both the people and the Emperor. From the day Telemachus fell dead, no other fight of gladiators was ever held.[11]

A Culture of Life

Christianity introduced an ethic which regarded every human life as sacred, because we are made in the image of God. John Ling points out that Western human medicine combined the best of Greek medicine, as summed up in the Hippocratic Oath, and the Judeo-Christian ethic of life as laid out in Scripture. 'For well over two thousand years, these two grand pillars have underpinned medical ethics and medical practice.'[12] These two millennia represented the 'Golden Age of Medicine', when medical care rested on the solid foundation of respect for life as given by God. But that solid foundation has been undermined. The British Medical Association proposed in 1997 to revise the Hippocratic Oath to allow for the killing of unborn human life.

A Culture of Death

Once a society rejects the belief that all human life has been created by God with unique dignity because we are made in the image of God, the door is open to a utilitarian system of

---

11   John Foxe, *Book of Martyrs*, Chapter 3, 'The Last Roman Triumph', https://www.ccel.org/f/foxe/martyrs/fox103.htm (accessed 29 April, 2020).

12   John R. Ling, *Bioethical Issues*, (Day One, 2014), p. 23.

ethics. There is then an easy progression to arguing that the 'less fit' should be eliminated.

The theory of evolution and the resulting naturalistic world view sees humans as the product of chance in an impersonal universe. But one implication of that is to deny the intrinsic dignity of every human life. The value of life begins to be assessed by criteria such as usefulness, enjoyment, or awareness.

Leo Alexander, an American doctor, attended the War Crimes tribunal at Nuremberg. He later wrote:

> Whatever proportions these crimes finally assumed, it became evident to all who investigated that they had started from small beginnings. The beginnings at first were merely a subtle shift in emphasis in the basic attitude of the physicians. It started with the acceptance of the attitude, basic in the euthanasia movement, that there is such a thing as a life not worthy to be lived.[13]

In 1980 a landmark book and film series *Whatever happened to the Human Race?*[14] was produced by Christian apologist **Francis Schaeffer (1912-1984)** and prominent doctor, **C. Everett Koop, (1916-2013)**. They argued that the idea of natural selection removed any logical belief in the unique value of human life, which opened the way to abortion, infanticide and euthanasia. The logical outworking of the

---

13 Leo Alexander, 'Medical Science under Dictatorship', *New England Journal of Medicine*, 241, (2) pp 39-47. https://www.nejm.org/doi/full/10.1056/NEJM194907142410201 (accessed 17 April, 2020).

14 Francis Schaeffer and C. Everett Koop, *Whatever happened to the Human Race?* (Marshall, Morgan and Scott, 1980).

theory of natural selection is the science of eugenics, selecting the best and fittest to breed.

The science of eugenics first emerged in Britain in the mid-nineteenth century, as an offshoot of Darwinism. It was embraced in the United States and elsewhere. Eugenicists wanted to improve public health by increasing births amongst the 'fit' and decreasing births amongst the 'unfit'. During the first decades of the twentieth century, more than thirty states in America adopted compulsory sterilisation laws. Individuals were forcibly sterilised because they were disabled, or ill, or belonged to socially disadvantaged groups. These policies could only be adopted because they secured public approval. Although some Christians opposed them, all too many were swept along:

> In America the evangelical mainstream in the decades following the turn of the century appeared apathetic, acquiescent, or at times downright supportive of the eugenics movement ... [they] often accepted eugenics as part of a progressive, reformist vision that uncritically fused the Kingdom of God with modern civilization.[15]

Tragically also there were racist undercurrents driving eugenics policies. The sterilisation rate among blacks was forty-five per cent higher than among whites; and among Hispanics it was thirty per cent higher. The notion of eugenics was

---

15 D. L. Durst, 'Evangelical Engagements with Eugenics, 1900 – 1940', *Ethics and Medicine: An International Journal of Bioethics*, Vol. 18.2, 2009, https://www.questia.com/library/journal/1P3-236342561/ evangelical-engagements-with-eugenics-1900-1940 (accessed 27 March, 2020).

discredited during and after World War II amidst revulsion at Nazi atrocities, and one by one the various American states abandoned the practice.

So history shows that Christians can be deceived by the claims of 'science' into endorsing medical 'ethics' which undermine the sanctity of human life. The same happened in both Britain and the United States when many evangelicals failed to speak out strongly against the introduction of abortion (abortion was, in effect, legalised in Britain in 1967 and in America in 1973).

While many Catholics had a clear understanding of the humanity and dignity of unborn life, many Protestants, including evangelicals, believed the 'experts' and assumed that support of abortion (in certain circumstances) was the 'compassionate' thing to do. Only when the appalling scale of the destruction of unborn life became apparent, did an evangelical pro-life movement gain momentum. *Whatever Happened to the Human Race?* proved a significant catalyst, and inspired many to join the pro-life movement. It provided a wake-up call and a warning: if the professed Church abandons confidence in absolute biblical morality, the effects can be disastrous.

Today we look back and lament evangelical failure to oppose abortion when permissive legislation was introduced. We see the terrible consequences: nine million abortions have taken place in Great Britain since 1967. In 2017 it was reckoned that there had been one billion babies killed by abortion worldwide in the past 100 years.[16] When we reflect that every human life from conception is priceless in worth, because made in the image of God, we tremble at the magnitude of that.

Today the demand for complete individual 'autonomy' has led to the claim that abortion is a 'human right'. It is assumed that women are only truly 'free' if they can rid themselves of an unwanted unborn child. This ignores the humanity of the child. Far from being 'free', many women have been, and are, pushed into having abortions. They may carry that burden with them for decades without relief. The Christian message offers hope and healing to such women.[17] Many Christians have supported holistic pro-life work, providing support and care for mothers as well as babies. For example, in the UK since 1970, LIFE has advocated the rights of unborn babies; provided housing and other support for mothers; and founded hospices for terminally ill infants and children.[18]

---

16 'Greatest genocide in history': Groundbreaking report finds 1 billion abortions in past 100 years', *LifeSite News*, https://www.lifesitenews.com/news/breaking-researchers-estimate-1-billion-abortions-globally-over-past-100-ye (accessed 29 April, 2020).

17 Many have found help through a Bible study programme which can be offered on a confidential basis, www.surrenderingthesecret.com (accessed 29 April, 2020).

18 https://lifecharity.org.uk/the-charity/history/ (accessed 3 November, 2020). This positive vision of care for both mother and baby is truly 'pro-life'. Sadly, some well-intentioned but over zealous campaigners adopt angry or confrontational messages or methods, but these do not reflect the compassion of Christ. See A. Johnstone, *Unplanned: The Dramatic True Story of a Former Planned Parenthood Leader's Eye-Opening Journey across the Life Line* (Focus on the Family, 2010).

In 1980, *Whatever Happened to the Human Race?* warned about other threats to the dignity of human life. Five years earlier, utilitarian ethicist and philosopher Peter Singer had published *Animal Liberation*. Regarding human life as sacred, Singer argued, is 'species-ism'. He said that it may be compassionate to kill unwanted unborn infants, newborns with disabilities or the incapacitated sick and elderly, just as it may be compassionate to kill suffering animals:

> Actions causing pain or destruction of sentient beings (i.e. beings with intelligent awareness, whales, for example) are wrong, but similar actions upon non-sentient beings (i.e. beings with seemingly no intelligent awareness, e.g. human embryos) are not wrong. The killing of disabled babies is justified in view of their likely suffering ...[19]

Three years before Schaeffer's book and film series, a book called *Ecoscience: Population, Resources, Environment* had been published.[20] The underlying message was that humans are bad for the planet. Government power may need to be extended to enable forced sterilisation, abortion, eugenics, and punitive carbon taxes. One of the authors, John P. Holdren, would later be appointed as senior advisor on science and technology to President Barack Obama.

Increasingly, some in the so-called 'deep green' or radical environmentalist movement argued that the earth itself is the

---

19 Phillip Singer, quoted in Simon Smart (ed), *A Spectator's Guide to World Views* (Blue Bottle Books, 2007), p. 92.

20 Paul Ehrlich, Anne H. Ehrlich, John P. Holdren, *Ecoscience: Population, Resources, Environment* (W. H. Freeman, 1977).

'greatest good', and that it is threatened by human life. Finnish activist, Pentti Linkola (1932–2020), for example, believed that humans are like a tumour on the earth, consuming more than our fair share of nature's resources. The vast majority of humans should be killed. The remainder should be controlled by an authoritarian environmentalist state, with people forcibly sterilized and private cars confiscated. His books have been best-sellers in Finland. His writing betrays a denial of human dignity:

> ... humanity, by squirting and birthing all these teeming, filth-producing multitudes from out of itself, in the process also suffocates and defames its own culture ...[21]

With that view of humanity, we are not surprised to know that, shockingly, he asked:

> Who misses all those who died in the Second World War? Who misses the twenty million executed by Stalin? Who misses Hitler's six million Jews?[22]

Mercifully there is, as yet, sufficient collective memory of the Christian world-view to prevent whole-sale acceptance of that human-hating philosophy. But how long will that memory last?

In a culture where 'absolute' morals are rejected, bioethics flails around in situation ethics: 'what do you feel about

---

21 Pentti Linkola, *Human Flood*, 1989, translated by H. Heinonen and M. Moynihan http://www.penttilinkola.com/pentti_linkola/ecofascism_writings/humanflood/ (accessed 26 March, 2020).

22 Ibid.

it?' Serious ethical issues such as 'embryo wastage', embryo experimentation, use of donor gametes in assisted reproduction, abortion, assisted suicide or euthanasia are seen as simply matters of personal choice.[23] In 2011 The *Journal of Medical Ethics* published an article arguing the case for aborting newborn infants:

> If criteria such as the costs (social, psychological, economic) for the potential parents are good enough reasons for having an abortion even when the foetus is healthy, if the moral status of the newborn is the same as that of the foetus and if neither has any moral value by virtue of being a potential person, then the same reasons which justify abortion should also justify the killing of the potential person when it is at the stage of a newborn.[24]

If humans are not created in God's image, then there is no certain defence against this argument. For in that case it is logical to seek the greatest good of the greatest number, and society could have an *obligation* to use abortion, infanticide, euthanasia and eugenic policies to regulate world population.

Christians through history have defended the sanctity of all human life. At this moment in history, we need to hold firm to the biblical truth that God created men and women in His own image.

---

23 For a comprehensive treatment of current threats to the sanctity of human life, see John Ling, *Bioethical Issues* (Day One, 2014).

24 A. Giubilini, and F. Minerva, 'After Birth Abortion, why should the Baby Live?' *Journal of Medical Ethics*, 2011, https://jme.bmj.com/content/39/5/261.full (accessed 26 March 2020).

Every Human Life Is Precious

In 1976, Vishal Mangalwadi and his wife Ruth moved back to his father's village, Gatheora in Chhatarpur District, Central India. They started a non-profit organisation to serve the rural poor in that area. Vishal recounts the time they tried to save the life of a little neighbour girl. The parents resisted all their efforts. They wanted the child to die. She was just one more mouth to feed. He writes:

> Before we knew it, Sheela was dead. Sheela's parents starved her to death because they saw her as a liability. They already had a daughter to babysit their sons and to clean and cook for the family. A second girl was an unnecessary burden. They would have to feed her for ten to twelve years. Then they would need to go into debt to find a dowry to marry her off. Her in-laws might torture her to extract more money from them... But a dowry is not the end of costs. The daughter would return to her parents' home to deliver her children. Why should they take on this lifelong burden, even if someone was offering [their little girl] free medical care and milk for a few weeks?[25]

Ruth and Vishal intervened because they believed every child had a fundamental right to life. 'We did not expect to gain anything from Sheela. We believed that loving God required loving her.'[26] By contrast:

---

25 Vishal Mangalwadi, *The Book that Made your World* (Thomas Nelson, 2011), p. 63.

26 Ibid.

Our neighbours did not understand [Ruth's] compassionate impulse because three thousand years of Hinduism, twenty-six hundred years of Buddhism, a thousand years of Islam, and a century of secularism had collectively failed to give them a convincing basis for recognizing and affirming the unique value of a human being.[27]

Respect for every human life did not arise from the other world religions, or from secularism. It arose from the biblical conviction that God created man and woman in His own image, and that Christ's incarnation, death, and resurrection forever confirmed the dignity, value and worth of the human condition.

Remember Telemachus and his lonely witness in the great Roman arena? When he heard the roars of the crowd, and realised that people made in God's image were being killed for entertainment, he was cut to the heart. He couldn't stay quiet. *'In the name of Christ, Stop!'* he cried.

That is a reminder to us to have courage to raise our voice when we see precious lives made in God's image being treated with contempt. Today the uniqueness and dignity of human life are often either openly denied or subtly undermined. We need to remain faithful in bearing witness to that foundational biblical truth.

---

27   Ibid., p. 72.

Further Reading

John R. Ling, *When does Human Life Begin?* The Christian Institute, https://www.christian.org.uk/wp-content/uploads/when-does-human-life-begin.pdf

Vishal Mangalwadi, *The Book that Made your World: How the Bible Created the Soul of Western Civilisation* (Thomas Nelson, 2011), pp. 59-76.

Alvin J. Schmidt, *How Christianity Changed the World* (Zondervan, 2004), pp. 48-76.

5 The Dignity of Women

Lal's life was wretched. Little more than a slave, a member of the 'Dalit' class, she lived in Pasrur (now Pakistan). She was despised as 'untouchable', and demeaned as a woman. Then she became a follower of Jesus Christ. Full of joy, she declared: *'Christ gave me honour in place of shame.'*[1]

Maliga lives in Banglur slum in Bangalore, one of the largest slums in India. In 2013 she testified: *'I tried to kill myself three times. A sister took me to church. I met Jesus. I am here today.'*[2]

Radical feminists accuse Christianity of oppressing women. Theologian Daphne Hampson, for example, claims that Christianity is irretrievably sexist, a dangerous male

---

1   Rebecca S. Shah, 'Christianity among the marginalized: Empowering Poor Women in India', *Christianity and Freedom*, vol. 2 (CUP, 2016), p. 107.

2   Ibid.

cultural projection, only constructed in order to legitimise a 'patriarchal world'.[3] Nothing could be further from the truth.

As far as the dignity of women is concerned, the birth of Jesus Christ was the most significant turning point in human history. His life, death and resurrection began the process of the rolling back of the judgement on sin pronounced in Genesis 3.16, *'Your desire will be for your husband and he will rule over you.'* Feminists are right to be outraged by abuse and violence against women. God is infinitely more angry at such sin. His good design for men and women was wrecked at the Fall, and both men and women are sinners. Over the past two thousand years, the true followers of Jesus Christ have borne witness to the truth that all human beings are to be treated with dignity and respect.[4]

The Early Church

At the time the New Testament was written, fathers routinely gave away their daughters as child-brides. Men could force their wives to have abortions, or they were forced to abandon sick or disabled or female newborn babies (see chapter four). There was no expectation that husbands should be faithful to their wives. It was commonplace for free men to use both male and female slaves for sexual gratification. In addition, they would expect to have mistresses.

---

3   Daphne Hampson, 'Luther on the Self: A Feminist Critique', pp. 215-25, in *Feminist Theology: A Reader*, ed. A. Loades (SPCK, 1990), p. 215.

4   Much of this chapter is taken from Sharon James, *God's Design for Women in an Age of Gender Confusion* (Evangelical Press, 2019), chapter 1.

In this context, Paul's insistence on a single standard of morality for men and women (1 Cor. 7:1-6), and his call for husbands to love and care for their wives (Eph. 5:25-33) was revolutionary. Demands for chastity outside of marriage and fidelity within marriage were just as outrageous and countercultural in the first century as they are today. Such demands were liberating and life-giving compared with the exploitation and abuse suffered by so many at that time.

The early Christians lived in a culture where a small, privileged elite of males had sexual access to the rest of the population. This ubiquitous culture of abuse created an ocean of exploitation and suffering. When God's norms for sexual morality and family life break down, women and children suffer most. Roman sexual culture rested on a bedrock of coercion. The poorest men who didn't have free access to their own slaves could hire prostitutes for pathetically low sums. Vile abuse surrounded the 'sex trade':

> The commodification of sex was carried out with all the ruthless efficiency of an industrial operation, the unfree body bearing the pressures of insatiable market demand. In the brothel the prostitute's body became, little by little, 'like a corpse'.[5]

The Christian sexual ethic forbade the buying and selling of sex. It held men and women to an equal standard. It gave equal dignity to husband and wife. This was revolutionary.

---

5   Kyle Harper, *From Shame to Sin: The Christian Transformation of Sexual Morality in Late Antiquity* (Harvard University Press, 2013), p. 49.

By contrast to Christian behaviour, the second-century poet and satirist Juvenal portrayed a society in which large numbers of people were dangerously addicted to ever more extreme sexual behaviour. Nothing was shameful or out of bounds.[6] Stage plays celebrated incest, physical torture for gratification, paedophilia and bestiality. The early Christians were counter-cultural in opposing such decadence. They did so because they believed that the dignity of each person made in God's image should be respected. And they knew that the faithful God calls for marriage promises to be honoured. So the Christian insistence on marital fidelity served to protect women, as did the prohibition of arbitrary divorce. Christians opposed the practice of marrying off young girls. When Constantine became Emperor, he initiated legal protections for women and marriage.[7]

Women began to secure property rights, and received the right of guardianship over their children (who before had been seen as the possession of men).[8] Because of Christian influence, in 374 the Emperor Valentinian repealed the one-thousand-year-old *patria potestas*: husbands lost the right of life and death over their family including their wives.[9] The accompanying cultural practices which placed married

---

6   Alvin J. Schmidt, *How Christianity Changed the World* (Zondervan 2004), p. 82.

7   Diana Lynn Severance, *Feminine Threads* (Christian Focus, 2011), p. 66.

8   Ibid., p. 67.

9   Schmidt, p. 111.

women under the husband's absolute rule, and gave a father the right to sell his daughter to her husband, also declined.

Sexual immorality was condemned. Radically, the one exploiting the prostitute was counted as guilty. Where a slave was coerced against their will, Basil of Caesarea assured them that they would be shown mercy by God because people lacking volition cannot be held responsible for the acts to which they were subjected.[10] Basil's concern for victims of prostitution resulted in imperial legislation to eliminate the practice. In 428 AD the Eastern Emperor (**Theodosius II**) proclaimed that those who had been trapped in prostitution should be helped out, given alternative means of living, and *not* penalised for what they were coerced into doing. Those who had coerced them, whether slave owners, fathers or pimps, should be punished:

> Pimps ... will be proscribed by exile to the public mines, which is less of a punishment than that of a woman who is seized by a pimp and compelled to endure the filth of an intercourse that she did not will.[11]

This was the first time that everyone, whatever their social status or lack of it, could claim protection from sexual predators. During the next century, the **Emperor Justinian** (Eastern Roman Emperor 527 to 565 AD) commissioned a special task force to investigate the use of coercion in the sex industry in Constantinople. He actively sought to repress

---

10   Harper, in *Christianity and Freedom*, Volume 1, pp. 137-8.

11   Ibid., p. 138.

sexual exploitation in his empire. He and his wife Theodosia financed a refuge for reformed prostitutes.[12]

The Spread of Christianity

When significant numbers of people in any community live according to Christian ethics, it has a positive impact on the lives of women. Over the centuries, as Christian missionaries travelled to proclaim the gospel, many challenged the oppression and lack of opportunity suffered by women and girls. One of the first indicators of Christian influence was the provision of education for girls as well as boys.

The first female missionary to the Far East from America was **Ann Judson (1789-1826)**, who left all she knew in America to sail for Burma in 1813. With her husband she pioneered Christian mission in Burma, but she especially focused on educating girls. Ann believed that Christian education for women was the means by which Asian females could be liberated from what was all too often a degraded and miserable life. In 1822 she published a powerful and widely read address to the women of America, in which she challenged them to give sacrificially to support female education in the East. Her appeal had huge impact in terms of funds and volunteers. When Ann died prematurely in Burma, her death inspired many other women to volunteer in the cause.[13]

Another Christian who devoted her life to female education was **Fidelia Fiske (1816-1864)**. In 1843 she travelled from America to Persia (now Iran) to pioneer female education.

---

12   Ibid., pp. 138-9.

13   Sharon James, *Ann Judson* (Evangelical Press, 2015).

She saw the provision of good schools for girls as the only way out of female oppression:

> The women were regarded by the men as drudges and slaves, and were compelled to spend most of the time in outdoor labour, among the vineyards and wheat-fields, often going out to work carrying not only their heavy implements, but also their babies. When, at evening, they returned from the fields, however weary, they had to milk the cows, prepare their husband's meal, and wait till he had finished before having any food themselves. It was commonplace for husbands to beat their wives brutally ... [14]

After sixteen years she had established a successful school for girls, and the lives of many women had been transformed. Fidelia's health was broken and she returned to America, where she continued to promote female education.

William Carey (1761-1834) is often regarded as the 'father of modern missions'. Although the British government specifically forbade the entry of missionaries to India, he and his fellow missionaries ministered in the early nineteenth century in the Danish territory of Serampore in Southern India. Among many other social reforms they set up the first schools for girls. By means of female education they hoped to break the practice of marrying off little girls from infancy onwards. If women were educated and able to earn a living, that would break the practice of widow burning, which was practised partly because widows were regarded as an economic

---

14 D. T. Fiske, *The Cross and the Crown; or, Faith Working by Love: The Life of Fidelia Fiske, missionary to Persia 1843-1858* (reprinted by Tentmaker Publications, 2005), pp. 91-2.

liability (they were forbidden to earn a living, *and* forbidden to remarry). The practice of sati involved the widow sacrificing herself by sitting or lying on top of her husband's funeral pyre. William Carey campaigned ceaselessly against the practice of widow burning. Many of the widows who died in this way were pitifully young. Carey conducted rigorous research, and publicised what was going on. One of his great allies in England was William Wilberforce. It took twenty-five years before the campaign against widow burning was successful. Often during that period Wilberforce would insist on reading out the names of widows who had been killed in this way during family breakfast before family prayers. The practice was finally made a criminal offence in 1829.

In 1987, Roop Kanwar, a 'bubbly' eighteen-year-old woman, committed sati in India. It was claimed this was entirely voluntary. She was widely praised. A shrine to honour her quickly received $160,000 in donations. In 2019, people were still flocking to honour the shrine.[15] In recent years in India there has been a resurgence of widow burning. It is claimed that this is voluntary, the widow's conscience tells her she should to preserve her honour and that of her family. Many today say that people should be free to do as they choose. William Carey insisted that we do not have that choice, because God, the giver of life, gives value to every human life.

---

15   A. Salik, 'Thirty Two Years after Roop Kanwar's Death Blind Faith Still overshadows Reason', *Outlook*, 21 October, 2019, https://www.outlookindia.com/magazine/story/india-news-thirty-two-years-after-roop-kanwars-death-blind-faith-still-overshadows-reason/302221 (accessed 27 March, 2020).

For Carey, the relevant question was not whether or not sati was a voluntary act:

> ... a woman's life was neither her own, nor her husband's. It was God's. And the Creator had not given to us the right to violate his gift of life.[16]

Christians also led the way in opposing foot-binding in China, which was only banned in 1912.[17] Christian missionaries in various countries tried to protect girls from female genital mutilation (FGM), or female cutting. This is still common in many countries, but it is absolutely condemned in countries which have historically been permeated with a Christian world view.[18]

Josephine Butler (1828-1906) fought *for* female education and employment, and *against* the sexual exploitation of women, in Britain and beyond. During the nineteenth century Josephine and her husband opened their home to provide shelter and a way out of prostitution for desperate women. She believed that prostitution was an evil which should not be regulated or condoned, and she campaigned against the contagious diseases acts (which were designed to provide a 'safe' supply of prostitutes for the armed forces). She was fearless in fighting against the sexual exploitation of children, and successfully worked for the raising of the age of consent to sixteen. Josephine was motivated by her deep Christian faith.

---

16   Vishal and Ruth Mangalwadi, *Carey, Christ and Cultural Transformation* (OM Publishing, 1993), pp. 91-2.

17   Schmidt, pp. 118-9.

18   Ibid., pp. 119-21.

She believed that all people are equally created in the image of God and to be protected and respected.[19]

As Christianity spread rapidly in Latin America, Asia, and Africa during the twentieth century, this had a positive impact on women. Research in those areas where Christianity is growing fastest, shows that, as with the early church, the worth afforded to women is a significant factor. When poor women are converted and join the new evangelical churches, they join communities with a high view of the family, and an emphasis on male responsibility and fidelity. Their husbands are far less likely to squander family resources on drinking, gambling or prostitutes.[20]

Christianity Today

Women today worldwide do still suffer oppression. But the countries where women are held back, forbidden an education, married off as children, and subjected to systematic abuses such as honour killings and genital cutting are the countries where Christianity is disallowed. Most are Muslim-majority nations, but the country named as most dangerous for women is India, with around one billion Hindus.[21] There is a strong Christian minority there, around seventy-one million

---

19   Jennifer Davies, *The Age of Consent: A Warning from History. The Work of Josephine Butler*, (The Christian Institute, 2009), https://www.christian.org.uk/wp-content/uploads/aoc_warning.pdf (accessed 27 March, 2020).

20   Philip Jenkins, *The Next Christendom: The Coming of Global Christianity* (Oxford University Press, 2011), pp. 96-7.

21   'India's Shame', *The Times,* 27 June 2018, https://www.thetimes.co.uk/article/india-s-shame-5b7lzdg60 (accessed 14 September, 2018).

Christians; they are often those who are changing things for the better for women.

Baglur slum in the great city of Bangalore contains more than 150 churches, mostly Pentecostal or charismatic, all within one and a half square kilometres. When in-depth interviews were conducted with women of all religions living in Baglur, it became apparent that conversion to Christianity led to liberation from fatalism and hopelessness. Women of other faiths acknowledged that the Christian husbands are noticeably less abusive, more loving and more likely to take earnings home than squander them on drink or other women. Christian women are transformed in terms of attitude towards themselves, they have a new concept of value and dignity, they are confident to speak out against and resist abuse. They are motivated to work more, earn more, give more and save more. Many are enabled to improve the lives of their families.[22]

In 2010 the feminist publishing house Virago published *Half The Sky: How To Change The World*, which documented female oppression worldwide. The authors, liberal feminists, admit that Bible-believing Christians are to be found fighting against female oppression in the hardest places on earth. For only Christians are willing to devote a lifetime to ministry in those appalling conditions. Others volunteer short-term. But you need an eternal perspective to be willing to sacrifice your whole life.[23]

22　Rebecca S. Shah, in *Christianity and Freedom*, Volume 2, pp. 113-23.

23　Nicholas Kristof and Sheryl WuDunn, *Half the Sky: How to Change the World* (Virago, 2010), pp. 157-60.

Margaret Atwood's *The Handmaid's Tale* (1985) depicts a dystopian nightmare of sexual slavery as the product of religious fundamentalism. It portrays the enemy as 'patriarchy', and seems to confirm the radical feminist notion that Christianity is bad news for women.

The *reality* is that the sexual slavery endemic in the ancient world was *dispelled* by the advance of Christianity. Sexual slavery is advancing again today. Exact figures are disputed, but the International Labour Organisation estimates that there are around twenty-one million victims of human trafficking worldwide, and that human trafficking is a $150 billion industry.[24] That's not because of Christianity. It's fuelled by the global pornography industry, which Christians oppose.

Worldwide it's often Christians who are at the forefront of opposing trafficking and slavery. For example, Christians in The Dignity Freedom Network in India work to liberate those trapped in slavery and the sex trade, many of whom are in the 'Dalit' caste.[25]

Bindya, for example, was born in the red-light district of the economic hub of India, Mumbai. The area was home to only women and children. Men only visited to buy sex. Bindya's mother died of HIV. Bindya was taken into a Christian rehabilitation centre which helps women and girls leave the life of prostitution and break the cycle of sex trafficking. By the age of fifteen she was top of her class at school and she

---

24 Quoted in Daniel Darling, *The Dignity Revolution* (The Good Book Company, 2018), p. 112.

25 https://www.om.org/en/news/freeing-dalits (accessed 11 December, 2019).

has every hope of a meaningful future far from the red-light district.[26]

Bindya's life has been transformed for the better by the Christian gospel. So have the lives of countless other women, including Lal and Maliga (whose testimonies we noted at the beginning of this chapter).

In God's eyes, every human made in His image is of priceless worth. Christianity is good news for women.[27]

Further Reading

Matthew Rueger, *Sexual Morality in a Christless World* (Concordia, 2016), pp. 11-41.

Alvin J. Schmidt, *How Christianity Changed the World* (Zondervan, 2004), pp. 97-122.

Rebecca S. Shah, 'Christianity among the marginalized: Empowering Poor Women in India', *Christianity and Freedom,* vol. 2 (CUP, 2016), pp. 107-32.

---

26   J. Weber, 'Freeing the Dalits', OM, https://www.om.org/en/news/freeing-dalits (accessed 27 March, 2020).

27   Sharon James, *God's Design for Women in an Age of Gender Confusion* (Evangelical Press, 2019).

6 Philanthropy

The searing image of five screaming children fleeing a napalm attack in Vietnam is regarded as one of the photographs that changed the world.[1] Kim Phuc recalls:

> On June 8, 1972, I ran out from Cao Dai temple in my village, Trang Bang, South Vietnam; I saw an airplane getting lower and then four bombs falling down. I saw fire everywhere around me. Then I saw the fire over my body, especially on my left arm. My clothes had been burned off by fire. I was 9 years old but I still remember my thoughts at that moment: I would be ugly and people would treat me in a different way. My picture was taken in that moment on Road No. 1 from Saigon to Phnom Penh. After a soldier gave me some drink and poured water over my body, I lost my consciousness.[2]

1   'Ten photographs that changed the world', (photo number 7), *Daily Telegraph*, 8 September, 2009, https://www.telegraph.co.uk/culture/ culturepicturegalleries/6152050/Ten-photographs-that-changed-the-world.html (accessed 17 April, 2020).

2   Kim Phuc, 'The Long Road to Forgiveness', *National Public Radio*, 30 June, 2008, https://www.npr.org/templates/story/story.php?storyId

Kim survived. She was left with terrible physical and psychological scars, and a heavy burden of anger, bitterness and hate. She was liberated from the bitterness, if not the physical pain, when she became a Christian. She testifies:

> Forgiveness made me free from hatred. I still have many scars on my body and severe pain most days, but my heart is cleansed.... [3]

Freed *from* hate, Kim Phuc was freed *to* love and serve. She has devoted her life to providing medical and psychological support to child victims of war. She is one of countless Christians who show love for God by showing love for their neighbour.

The whole Bible bears witness to the reality that our triune God is a God of mercy and compassion.

> The LORD is gracious and compassionate,
>> slow to anger and rich in love.
> The LORD is good to all;
>> he has compassion on all he has made. (Ps. 145:8-9)

God insists that anyone who wants to honour Him will have mercy on the needy (Prov. 14:31). He tells His followers that if we merely profess belief, but ignore the suffering, our faith is dead (James 2:14-17).

Compassion characterised the ministry of Christ:

> When Jesus landed and saw a large crowd, he had compassion on them and healed their sick. (Matt. 14:14)

=91964687&t=1587132565920 (accessed 17 April, 2020).

3   Ibid.

When Jesus was asked specifically how Christian love *(agape)* was to be shown, and to whom, He answered with the story of the Good Samaritan, and said, 'Go and do likewise' (Luke 10:25-37).[4] This self-giving love was a revolutionary concept. The account of the Good Samaritan has been described as the parable that changed the world.

Over the centuries, the followers of Christ have been at the forefront of efforts to relieve suffering and need. The West has a tradition of philanthropy and a culture of giving and sharing that is unmatched in any other civilisation in history. Today, whether or not we were brought up in Christian homes, we have been brought up in a culture which has been shaped by the Christian world view. We take for granted that 'compassion' is a good thing. But that assumption is not fundamental to cultures which have not been impacted by Christianity. Indian author Vishal Mangalwadi observes the contrast between the biblical ethic, and the Hindu concept of a hierarchical society where Brahmins are at the top and 'untouchables' are at the bottom.[5]

Compassion: A Revolutionary Concept

In pagan culture, compassion to the needy was often regarded as foolish. The Greeks regarded virtues as qualities such as strength, courage and self-control. Compassion was seen as a

---

4   Hugh Flemming, 'Post-Hippocratic Medicine: The Problem and the Solution: How the Christian Ethic has influenced Health Care'. *Kuyper Foundation*, 2010, https://www.kuyper.org/s/TextPost-HippocraticMedicine.pdf (accessed 17 April, 2020), p. 22.

5   Vishal Mangalwadi, *The Book that Made your World* (Thomas Nelson, 2011), p. 300.

weakness. Plato and others held that a poor man should be left to die, if he could no longer work:

> The heroes of the Iliad, favourites of the gods, golden and predatory, had scorned the weak and the downtrodden. So too ... had philosophers. The starving deserved no sympathy. Beggars were best rounded up and deported. Pity risked undermining a wise man's self-control. Only fellow citizens of good character, who through no fault of their own, had fallen on evil days might conceivably merit assistance.[6]

Certainly benevolence was held to be a virtue; people gave gifts. But something was generally expected in return. In the Roman Empire the most significant contribution to health care was the infrastructure improving public health, including water supplied to the great cities. Wealthy benefactors might contribute to public works, and would receive due public honour and recognition.

By contrast, Christians were widely noted for their compassion, and willingness to give without expectation of reward. Jesus taught His followers to love their enemies and show mercy to all. Paul wrote to the Christians at Colossae:

> Therefore, as God's chosen people, holy and dearly loved, clothe yourselves with compassion, kindness, humility, gentleness and patience. (Col. 3:12)

This message, lived out, resulted in radical communities which offered love and care. Pagans went to the temple to

---

6   Tom Holland, *Dominion: The Making of the Western Mind* (Little, Brown, 2019), p. 121.

make offerings. They didn't belong to a familial community. By contrast, the Church was the body of Christ. When one member suffered, all suffered.

This practical compassion was a major factor in rapid Church growth. In 40 AD, there were probably no more than a few thousand Christians. As mentioned in chapter four, by 350 AD there were possibly over thirty-three million Christians in the Roman Empire out of a total population of sixty million.[7] Rodney Stark describes how their ethic impacted the misery and brutality of life in the urban Greco-Roman world:

> To cities filled with the homeless and impoverished, Christianity offered charity as well as hope. To cities filled with newcomers and strangers, Christianity offered an immediate basis for attachments. To cities filled with orphans and widows, Christianity provided a new and expanded sense of family. To cities torn by violent ethnic strife, Christianity offered a new basis for social solidarity. And to cities faced with epidemics, fires and earthquakes, Christianity offered effective nursing services.[8]

Christian response to poverty was grounded in beliefs about human dignity. No pagan cult insisted that caring for the sick, the poor, widows and orphans was an essential religious duty.[9] A third-century Christian handbook, The *Didascalia*,

---

7   Rodney Stark, *The Rise of Christianity* (HarperCollins, 1997), p. 7.

8   Rodney Stark, *The Rise of Christianity: A Sociologist Reconsiders History* (Princeton University Press, 1996), p. 155.

9   David Bentley Hart, *Atheist Delusions: The Christian Revolution and its Fashionable Enemies* (Yale University Press, 2010), p. 164.

instructed church leaders to ensure that orphans receive education, widows obtain aid, and the destitute be given food and firewood.[10] By the middle of the third century, the Church at Rome was helping more than one thousand five hundred needy people. Even small churches kept storerooms of provisions for the poor: food, firewood, oil, wine and clothing. Once Constantine became emperor the Church became the first organised institution of public welfare in Western history.[11]

The early Christian apologist **Tertullian (c. 155–220 AD)** noted that donations given to pagan temples were often spent on gluttony and feasting. By contrast, Christians willingly gave to the Church and used the funds to support the poor, abandoned and elderly, and to provide a decent burial for those who couldn't afford one.[12]

The **Emperor Julian the Apostate (r. 361-363)** lamented that the Christians, whom he hated, showed love and compassion, famously saying: that the *'Galileans, to our disgrace, support not only their poor but ours.'*[13] He believed that the Christians' sacrificial kindness towards strangers had been a major factor in the spread of their beliefs.

---

10   Ibid., p. 164.

11   Ibid., pp. 163-4.

12   Ibid., p. 164.

13   Ibid., p. 191. 'Galileans' was Julian's derogatory way of speaking of Christians.

Philanthropy in the Middle Ages

During the middle ages both clergy and laity contributed to, and served in, various ministries for the poor and the sick.[14] Leper houses could be found across Europe. Willingness to provide care for the destitute was regarded as a mark of true devotion to Christ. To engage in charitable deeds was to imitate Christ. Many believed that by caring for the needy, they could, in a mystical way, care for Christ Himself.

Lay people as well as monks and nuns devoted themselves to working in refuges for the poor or the lepers. One noble woman who did the same was the Hungarian Princess **Elizabeth (1207-1231)**, who founded a hospital for the poor at Marburg, and visited daily to provide care for the destitute.

Another woman celebrated for deeds of mercy was **Catherine of Siena (1347-1380)**. She was born in Tuscany, the twenty-fourth of twenty-five children. The year after her birth, the Black Death reached Europe. It killed around a third of the continent's population. Catherine survived, and grew up to devote much of her life to the poor and the ill. In 1374 another outbreak of plague struck her home town of Siena. She, along with other pious Christians, remained to nurse the sick and bury the dead. Catherine is remembered today for her mystical experiences of the love of Christ, but she believed

---

14   A. J. Davis, 'The Charitable Revolution', *Christian History,* 101, 2011, 'Healthcare and Hospitals', https://christianhistoryinstitute.org/magazine/article/charitable-revolution (accessed 20 April, 2020).

that experiential love for God cannot be separated from practical love for neighbour.[15]

In 1370 a wealthy layman asked the Augustinian author Walter Hilton for advice on how he could express his new-found love for Christ. Hilton wrote him a series of letters with practical instructions on the 'mixed life': how to combine ordinary working life with nurturing warm devotion and performing practical deeds of mercy:

> Don't spend all your time meditating on the Passion to the neglect of your fellow Christians. Wash Christ's feet by attending to your subjects and your tenants.[16]

The Evangelical Awakenings: An Outpouring of Philanthropy

The great revivals of the eighteenth century in Great Britain, America and beyond were sparked off by earlier renewal movements on the continent of Europe. Mainstream reformers such as Luther had introduced biblical reform with regard to salvation. But they maintained the belief that all the infants in a given territory should be baptised into the national Church. This inevitably led to the nominalism and spiritual decline of second and third generation Christianity. Luther's doctrine of 'salvation by grace' alone became a doctrine of 'cheap grace'. By the seventeenth century Lutheran ministers reported:

---

15 C. T. Marshall, 'Catherine of Siena', 'Women in the Mediaeval Church', *Christian History,* 30, 1991, pp. 8-11.

16 Walter Hilton, Epistle on the Mixed Life, quoted in D. L. Jeffrey, *The Law of Love: English Spirituality in the Age of Wyclif* (Eerdmans, 1988), pp. 229-35.

Those who come to service are usually drunk . . and sleep through the whole sermon, except sometimes they fall off the benches making a great clatter, or women drop their babies on the floor ... They play cards while the pastor preaches, and often mock or mimic him cruelly to his face ... cursing and blaspheming, hooliganism and fighting are common.[17]

Those Christians who called the Church back to a biblical faith and walk were often known as 'Pietists'. One of their leaders was **Auguste Hermann Francke (1663-1727)**.

As a young university student, Francke struggled to find direction in life. In his autobiography he wrote:

For twenty-four years ... I loved the world and the world loved me... I grasped heaven with one hand and the earth with the other, I wanted fellowship with God and the friendship of the world at the same time, and could hold neither properly.[18]

But then he was converted. In 1692 he became both a pastor, and a professor of Oriental Studies at the newly established Halle University (in what is now central Germany). Over the next twenty years, he taught generations of pastors, emphasising a changed life. He was himself an exceptionally active pastor. He preached five times a week, held daily catechism classes for young people, published a religious magazine and promoted world missions. Under his leadership at Halle, the believers provided an orphanage, two homes for

---

17   Rodney Stark, *Bearing False Witness* (SPCK, 2017), p. 211.

18   August H. Francke, 'An Autobiography', 1692, Quoted in *Christian History,* 'The Pietists', pp. 7, 8, 33.

widows, free food for needy students, a home for beggars, job creation schemes for the unemployed, free medicine for the poor, and care for the physically disabled.

Francke was fearless in speaking truth to power. When he was called on to preach at the funeral of the ruler, Friedrich I, he declared to the grandees, nobles and politicians present: 'You, the mighty, the ruling and the wealthy are truly pitiable people if you do not have the Spirit of God',[19] and he reminded them of their duty to care for all their citizens.

The motto of the pietists was 'God's glory and neighbour's good'. The two went together. They believed in social engagement as an outflow of love for neighbour.

It was through the witness of some of those continental evangelicals that two Church of England clergymen, John and Charles Wesley, came to real living faith.

Whenever God has moved to revive the Church, there has been ethical fruit, an outpouring of mercy and compassion. That is certainly the case when we look at the evangelical awakenings of the eighteenth and nineteenth centuries. Despite opposition, many were born again, their lives were transformed, and the evangelical revival inspired a nationwide moral reformation and outpouring of mercy ministries. The awakenings in Britain and America created a whole culture where 'benevolence', 'sympathy', 'compassion' and 'fellow-feeling' became a social ethos which found expression in numerous reform movements and philanthropic enterprises. The tone of public life was elevated. Public hanging, which

---

19   https://christianhistoryinstitute.org/magazine/article/moving-on-many-fronts (accessed 23 December, 2019).

had become a form of mass entertainment, was ended. So-called 'asylums' for the mentally ill had been opened to provide amusement for the general public, this ended too.

By contrast, in France a more aggressively secular enlightenment resulted in Revolution, but the revolutionaries did little to improve the lives of the poor. Historian Gertrude Himmelfarb argues that the French philosophers produced neither the community of philanthropists nor the multitude of private societies that were so prominent in Britain.[20] The poor were worse off at the end of the French Revolution than at the beginning.

A second Great Awakening at the end of the eighteenth century and continuing through the nineteenth century, led to tens of thousands more people on both sides of the Atlantic converting to living Christianity. Evangelical Christians were responsible for a remarkable range of social reforms: prison reform, care of the mentally ill, factory reform, rescuing women and children from sexual abuse, provision of education, and of course, the abolition of the slave trade.

By the mid-nineteenth century, according to historian Owen Chadwick, evangelical religion 'seemed suddenly to be the most potent religious and moral force in England'.[21] Probably three-quarters of the total number of voluntary charitable organisations in Britain during the second half of

---

20 Gertrude Himmelfarb, *The Roads to Modernity: The British, French and American Enlightenments* (Vintage, 2008), p. 181.

21 Owen Chadwick, *The Victorian Church,* Part 1 (A&C Black, 1966), p. 454.

the nineteenth century were evangelical.[22] Large numbers of laymen and women gave time, energy and money to help an extraordinary variety of organisations reaching out to help street children, prostitutes, orphans, prisoners, the sick and disabled, and other needy people.

William Wilberforce's role in opposing slavery is well known (see chapter one). But he also longed to see wider spiritual and moral reformation. He wanted nominal Christianity to be transformed into living Christianity. His book *A Practical View of Christianity* (1797) became a bestseller, and was one of the catalysts of the second evangelical revival. Wilberforce urged that if a Christian had any free time, particularly on the Lord's Day, he or she should diligently throw their energies into:

> ... relieving the needy, visiting the sick, comforting the sorrowful, and forming plans for the good of their fellow creatures ...[23]

A dynamic group of evangelicals, active between about 1790 and 1830, based in Clapham, South London, pioneered an astonishing range of enterprises in education, moral reform in society, care for the needy, campaigning against slavery, and promoting mission work, evangelism and Bible translation. They gave generously, set up societies, and campaigned and lobbied in Parliament. Members included Hannah More (see

---

22   Kathleen Heasman, *Evangelicals in Action* (Geoffrey Bles, 1962), p. 14.

23   William Wilberforce, *A Practical View of Christianity,* (ed.) K. C. Belmonte (Hendrickson Publishers, 1996), p. 104.

chapter eight), Zachary Macaulay, Granville Sharp, James Stephen, and Henry Venn. Beyond this group, there were countless other 'entrepreneurs' in doing good. Some, such as Elizabeth Fry and the Earl of Shaftesbury, are still remembered today. Others, such as Thomas Jones and Sarah Martin, have long been forgotten.

Elizabeth Fry (1780-1845)

Elizabeth Gurney was born in 1780 into a wealthy Quaker family.[24] Converted as a teenager, she took the initiative to start a school for poor children in her neighbourhood. Having secured permission to use a large brick outhouse, she transformed it into her school-room. The children who attended were known in the neighbourhood as 'Betsy's imps'. Eventually there were eighty-six of them.

In 1800, Elizabeth had to leave her 'imps' when she married a fellow Quaker called Joseph Fry and moved to London. They went on to have eleven children, but Elizabeth still found time to do good. She first visited Newgate Prison in 1813.

The conditions horrified her. Prison conditions at this time were appalling. Jailers received no pay, and lived on bribes, tips, fees, extortions, and by organising prostitution. Many prisoners died of jail fever. Elizabeth found that many of the women in Newgate had never received a trial, but they were trapped in vile conditions with their children, and there was little hope of release. She started a school and

---

24 At that time many Quakers were Bible-believing non-conformists, many of them today would be liberal in theology.

organised employment schemes. Conditions in Newgate were transformed.

Elizabeth Fry was a major driving force behind new legislation to make the treatment of prisoners more humane. She was supported in her efforts by Queen Victoria. Elizabeth also opened a shelter in London for the homeless. In 1840 she opened a training school for nurses. Her programme inspired Florence Nightingale, who took a team of Fry's nurses to assist wounded soldiers in the Crimean War. Nightingale then went on to reform the entire nursing profession (see chapter seven).

Elizabeth Fry is still remembered as a leading reformer. A picture of her reading to prisoners at Newgate Prison appeared on the reverse of £5 notes issued between 2001 and 2016 by the Bank of England.

The Earl of Shaftesbury (1801-1885)

If you visit Piccadilly Circus, London, you will see The Shaftesbury Memorial, placed there to honour the philanthropic work of the seventh Earl of Shaftesbury. It features a statue of a winged archer depicting *The Angel of Christian Charity* (popularly, but wrongly, known as *Eros*). The seventh Earl of Shaftesbury was a great British politician, philanthropist and social reformer. As a little boy, he was miserably neglected by his own parents. But the family's evangelical housekeeper, Maria Mills, cared for him and showed him real Christ-like love. Partly due to Maria's influence, Shaftesbury grew up to became one of the leading evangelicals of his age. When he was twenty-six, he formulated his personal mission statement:

I want nothing but usefulness to God and my country.[25]

His first major political campaign was to fight for reform in the care of the mentally ill. He is more famous for his lead in reforms in the area of child labour and his work on behalf of chimney sweeps.[26] All this, and more, was inspired by his passion to obey Christ. One biographer suggested that:

> No man has ever done more to lessen the extent of human misery or to add to the sum total of human happiness.[27]

When Shaftesbury died, the streets of London were filled with poor people: flower-girls, boot-blacks, crossing-sweepers, factory-hands and many others who waited for hours to see his coffin pass by.

Thomas Jones (1752-1845)

Less well-known is the Welsh clergyman Thomas Jones. He was driven away from his parish church in Wales in 1785. He had been converted to genuine living Christianity, and the parishioners were embarrassed by his 'enthusiasm'. Eventually he became curate of a tiny hamlet of forty-six

---

25 Richard Turnbull, *Shaftesbury: The Great Reformer* (Lion, 2010), p. 24.

26 The Factory Act of 1833 limited number of working hours to 48 a week for children under 13; this was followed by three further Acts in 1864, 1867 and 1871. An Act was passed forbidding the use of boys in sweeping chimneys in 1840, but it was ineffective. Shaftesbury continued campaigning on their behalf, until an Act was passed in 1875 which finally eradicated the practice.

27 Georgina Battiscombe, *Shaftesbury: A Biography of the Seventh Earl. 1801–1885* (Constable, 1974), p. 334.

houses in Northamptonshire with an annual stipend of £25. He ministered faithfully in that obscure place for forty-three years.

From that humble base he transformed the surrounding community. He wrote devotional books in English and Welsh. All the profits were ploughed into charitable enterprises. He was the founder of Sunday schools, elementary schools, sick clubs and clothing clubs. He built six almshouses for aged widows. He founded an Education Society which enabled fifty Evangelical laymen to enter the ministry. He created the 'Society for Poor Pious Clergymen', and he raised funds to distribute more than £35,000 to clergy more needy than himself.[28] He did incalculable good.

Sarah Martin (1791-1843)

Another example of a now-forgotten Christian is Sarah Martin. Orphaned at an early age, she had gone out to work as a seamstress aged fourteen. In 1810, aged nineteen, she felt compelled to go into a chapel service in Great Yarmouth. That morning she heard a preacher expound 2 Corinthians 5:11: *'Since, then, we know what it is to fear the Lord, we try to persuade others.'* Sarah was converted, and testified:

I wished to give proof of my love, and desired the Lord to open privileges to me of serving my fellow creatures, that

---

28 John Wesley Bready, *England before and after Wesley* (Hodder and Stoughton, 1939), pp. 57-8.

happily I might, with the Bible in my hand, point others to those fountains of joy, whence my own so largely flowed.[29]

She continued to work long hours as a dressmaker. But she devoted every other waking hour to serving others: visiting those in the nearby workhouse hospital; providing schooling to poor children, teaching factory girls. When she was twenty-seven she began visiting prisoners in the Tolhouse Gaol in Great Yarmouth. Conditions were among the worst in the country. Men and women indiscriminately were crammed into two vile underground dungeons infested with rats and lice. At first, Sarah read the Bible to prisoners. She then organised Sunday services, began literacy classes, and introduced schemes for paid work. Eventually the town authorities were so delighted with improved conditions in the prison, and declining reoffending rates in the town, that they paid her to work full-time with the prisoners. Her health broke down as a result of her labours, and she died in 1843 aged fifty-two.[30]

Sarah Martin was just one of tens of thousands of Christians during the nineteenth century in England who expected to devote significant amounts of time in voluntary Christian service to those more needy than themselves. It was the expectation that genuine Christians would be engaged in active benevolence. It was taken for granted just as much as we might expect a genuine Christian to pray and read the Bible.

29 Frank Prochaska, *Women and Philanthropy in 19th Century England* (Clarendon Press, 1980), p. 165.

30 Matthew Pickhaver, 'Walking in good works – the Sarah Martin story', *Evangelical Times,* August 2015.

Industrialisation during the nineteenth century led to rapidly growing cities. The great challenges of urban poverty and spiritual need motivated William and Catherine Booth to establish the Christian Mission in London in 1865. It would later be known as the Salvation Army. A war was waged against the evils of poverty and godlessness by means of 'soup, soap and salvation'. Today there are Salvation Army branches in more than seventy-five countries, running missions, hospitals, emergency and disaster services, drug and alcohol rehabilitation programs and many other community projects.

Christian Philanthropy Upholding Family and the Work Ethic

In 1815, the remarkable theologian and political economist **Thomas Chalmers (1780–1847)** took up the ministry at the Tron Church in Glasgow. In 1819 he was transferred to the poorest parish in the city: an area of grim industrial slums, where people lived close-packed in utter squalor. Chalmers regarded any poor relief which created long-term dependency and destroyed morality as a 'moral gangrene'. It resulted in even more deeply entrenched poverty.[31] He set up a parish-based scheme, involving personal visits from elders and deacons, which sought to transform the spiritual and moral conditions of the parish, as well as the material circumstances.

Chalmers exemplified the tradition of Christian compassion and philanthropy which was founded on biblical truth. There was a recognition that love for neighbour

---

31   Robert Whelan, *The Corrosion of Charity: From Moral Renewal to Contract Culture* (Institute of Economic Affairs, 1996), p. 97.

impelled compassion for the needy. But while providing help, the creation principles found in Genesis 1 and 2 should not be undermined. Marriage and work are both part of God's design for humanity (Gen. 1:28). If well-intended provision of welfare has the *unintended* consequence of *discouraging* either stable family formation, or the work ethic, or both, it does more harm than good.

The married family serves not only to link past and future generations, and provide children with ongoing care from their natural families, it provides significant 'social capital' for communities. The sexual revolution led to a culture where individual freedom was viewed as all-important. Self-fulfilment was elevated; and the 'restrictions' of family norms denigrated. Increasingly welfare programmes worked to dis-incentivise marriage. As a result, we now see historically unprecedented global levels of fatherlessness. In 1964 only four small countries (Austria, Latvia, Iceland and Sweden) had more than ten per cent of children born outside marriage. By 2016, more than sixty per cent of children were born outside marriage in twenty-five countries. A further twenty countries, including Belgium, Denmark, Norway, France and Sweden had more than fifty per cent of children born outside marriage.[32]

Family breakup is a major factor behind the escalation of poverty, homelessness and mental health issues. James Bartholomew's book, *The Welfare of Nations,* cites detailed

---

32   Joseph Chamie, 'Out-of-wedlock births rise Worldwide', *Yale Global Online,* 16 March 2017, https://yaleglobal.yale.edu/content/out-wedlock-births-rise-worldwide (accessed 17 November, 2020).

evidence from eleven countries, showing that those welfare states which undermine the married family create new and lasting problems.[33] In this context, some Christians are at the forefront of charitable enterprises aimed at strengthening families, promoting reconciliation rather than separation.[34]

At lower income levels the way that taxes and benefits mesh together can destroy any incentive to work, which, perversely, only deepens poverty. James Bartholomew provides evidence from eleven countries to support his claim that:

> For the most part, the permanent mass unemployment of modern times has been caused by welfare states ... The permanently high unemployment that has been created has been highly damaging to the happiness of millions of people.... it has also caused collateral damage ... harming civility and honesty, weakening families and, of course, enfeebling economic growth.[35]

By contrast over the centuries Christian philanthropy recognised the human dignity of work. We have already noted the job-creation schemes pioneered by August Hermann Francke in Halle during the eighteenth century.

Today, many Christians in wealthier countries offer micro-loans to start one-person businesses, or invest in small or medium enterprises in poor countries, or give generously to

---

33 James Bartholomew, *The Welfare of Nations* (Biteback Publishing, 2017).

34 For example, the work of CARE for the Family, https://www. careforthefamily.org.uk/ (accessed 15 June, 2020).

35 Bartholomew, p. 46.

educational and training programmes.[36] All of these contribute to productivity which leads more quickly to a freedom from dependence (see chapter nine).

Intrinsic to the gospel itself is the gift of hope and dignity which motivates a future-orientated attitude and willingness to work hard. A study of poor women in Banglur slum in Bangalore found that when women converted to Christianity, they were liberated from fatalism and a hopeless attitude to the future. This launched them on a 'virtuous circle':

> A woman feels better, works more, and earns more money. The extra money earned and saved encourages the woman to earn more and to save more and to plan for future investment such as building a house or buying a refrigerator. An increase in income enables her to reach a 'tipping point' that can propel her out of the poverty trap and into more productive and future-orientated patterns of expenditure and saving.[37]

These women in Banglur also found dignity as they were able to give generously to those in greater need than themselves.

Christian compassion and philanthropy, when grounded in biblical truth, is also realistic about human nature. God has created people with the dignity of moral agency. There needs to be a safety net to protect the vulnerable. But policies offering long-term subsidies for self-destructive behaviour

---

36 Wayne Grudem, *Business for the Glory of God: The Bible's Teaching on the Moral Goodness of Business* (Crossway, 2003), p. 81.

37 Rebecca S. Shah, 'Christianity among the marginalized: Empowering Poor Women in India', *Christianity and Freedom* (CUP, 2016), vol. 2, p. 125.

disrespect human dignity and moral responsibility. There are long-term unintended harmful consequences.

Christian Compassion Extended to Concern for Animal Welfare

Evangelicals were also at the forefront of campaigning against cruelty to animals. Before the evangelical awakening of the eighteenth century, animals often suffered in the name of 'sport'. The baiting of bulls, bears and badgers, the teasing and torture of cats, dogs, rams, cocks and ducks were all commonplace. One sport was described in this way:

> A mad bull to be dressed up with fireworks and turned loose in the game place, a dog to be dressed up with fireworks over him, a bear to be let loose at the same time, and a cat to be tied to the bull's tail; a mad bull dressed up with fireworks to be baited.[38]

John Wesley and others denounced such cruelty. Wesley was well-known for showing kindness to the horses he rode in the course of his itinerant preaching ministry. He preached on the care of animals. He called on his followers to 'imitate Him whose mercy is over all His works'. He and the early Methodists also denounced widely acceptable practices like bull-baiting and cock-fighting.

In 1824 William Wilberforce and others founded what is now the Royal Society for the Prevention of Cruelty to Animals, the oldest animal welfare organisation in the world. Wilberforce's biblical conviction was that the creation

---

38 Bready, pp. 150-1.

mandate means stewarding creation on behalf of the Creator. God gave animals to humans for food, but He also forbids needless ill treatment, and He expects humans to show compassion for all living things.

Christian Compassion Today

Recently the Pew Research Center in America investigated the behaviour of a large sample of the public across a typical seven-day period. They found that of those who attended services weekly and prayed daily, forty-five per cent had done volunteer work during the previous week (compared with twenty-seven per cent of others). Between them, members of American churches and synagogues send four and a half times as much money overseas to needy people every year as the Gates Foundation:

> Much of this religious charity is applied in the hardest places, with high efficiency and low overhead, by Christians who 'go the last mile' into rural, extremely poor, or dangerous areas where governments and international bureaucracies have no effective reach.[39]

Local church congregations and larger para-church groups provide most of the day-to-day help that resettles refugees and asylum seekers arriving in the United States. A large proportion of the volunteers who mentor prisoners and their families are Christians. It has been found in one American

---

39 Karl Zinsmeister, 'Less God, Less Giving?' *Philanthropy Roundtable,* Winter 2019, https://www.philanthropyroundtable.org/philanthropy-magazine/less-god-less-giving (accessed 27 March, 2020).

study that shutting down a city congregation will often damage a neighbourhood's viability and socio-economic health. But active churches, religious schools, and church-based ministries have a positive impact on local communities. It isn't just a matter of doing good to others:

> People of faith also behave differently themselves. There is lots of evidence that in addition to encouraging a 'brother's keeper' attitude that manifests itself in philanthropy and volunteering, religious participation also inculcates healthy habits that help individuals resist destructive personal behaviour themselves.[40]

In the United Kingdom, it is estimated that evangelicals have formed as many charitable and philanthropic organisations since 1960 as had been established in the golden age of evangelical influence in the nineteenth century.[41] A 2003 Home Office Citizenship Survey calculated that a quarter of regular churchgoers, or around a million people, are involved in voluntary community service outside the church, concluding that people who follow a religion were significantly more likely to formally volunteer.[42] In 2006 a survey of the UK

---

40 Ibid.

41 Peter G. Brierley, *UK Christian Handbook,* 1985/6, pp. 365-75; 410-6; 421.

42 Nick Spencer, *Doing God: A future for faith in the public square,* Theos, p. 43, https://www.theosthinktank.co.uk/cmsfiles/archive/files/Reports/TheosBookletfinal.pdf (accessed December 11, 2019).

found that Christians give seven and a half times as much as others of their salary to charities, churches and good causes.[43]

Christian Compassion Internationally

Where the followers of Christ have gone, and where the followers of Christ are, there are people who are obeying Christ's commands to care for the needy. To take just one country as an example: Vietnam. Christians there have played, and still play, an outsized role in education, health, aid to the poor and vulnerable, and the upholding of human rights. In particular, by the end of the nineteenth century Roman Catholic missionaries had had a major social impact:

> From the 1880s ...missionaries began to found orphanages, hospitals, dispensaries, leper colonies, houses for the elderly and terminally ill, all of which were rare ...Such institutions introduced to Vietnam the concept of public welfare. These services, freely offered to non-Catholics, played an important part in meeting social needs ... and helping people conceptualize a more just and humane society.[44]

Right into the current century, evangelicals have played a major role in promoting the common good through relief, schools, clinics, hospitals and development projects. Where people convert to Christianity in Vietnam, it is demonstrated that they are motivated to make positive social contributions.

43 Quoted in Lynda Rose, (ed.), *What are they Teaching the Children?* (VFJ/Wilberforce Publications, 2016), p. 263.

44 Reg Reimer, 'Vietnam: Christianity's Contribution to Freedoms and Human Flourishing under Adversity', pp. 254-83, *Christianity and Freedom*, vol. 2, p. 261.

Importantly, also in Vietnam, Christian missionaries developed the romanised script which replaced the far more difficult character-based script. This made possible the achievement of an extremely high literacy rate, more than ninety-five per cent.[45]

We began this chapter with the story of a little Vietnamese girl whose life was changed forever by falling bombs. Kim Phuc has devoted her life to rehabilitating children whose lives, like hers, have been ruined by war. She knows that without Christ she would still be consumed with bitterness. Instead, she has the joy of serving others, and can testify:

> Napalm is very powerful; but faith, forgiveness and love are much more powerful.[46]

Further Reading

Vishal Mangalwadi, *The Book that made your World* (Thomas Nelson, 2011), pp. 298-308.

Alvin J. Schmidt, *How Christianity Changed the World,* (Zondervan, 2004), pp. 125-48.

---

45 Ibid.

46 Kim Phuc, *The Long Road to Forgiveness,* National Public Radio, 30 June, 2008, https://www.npr.org/templates/story/story.php?storyId=91964687&t=1587132565920 (accessed 17 April, 2020).

7 Healthcare

The letters 'CV' took on a new and sinister meaning at the end of 2019 as we heard of a new virus taking its toll in Wuhan, China. As journalists from around the world gathered at the front of Wuhan Central Hospital, few noticed the statue of the founder of the hospital – the Italian Roman Catholic Bishop Eustachius Zanoli.[1] And as medics fought to save patients in the neighbouring Wuhan Union Hospital, one of the best in Central China, few remembered that it had been founded by the Welsh Protestant missionary, Griffith John, in 1886.

Just a few decades before that, American Presbyterian missionary Peter Parker had founded China's first hospital (in the modern sense) in Guangzhou. It is now China's best-known ophthalmic institute. By the end of the nineteenth century, more than a hundred missionary-run hospitals in China had treated millions of patients. Researcher William Huang found that:

---

1   Chris Buckley from *The New York Times*. Zanoli founded the original hospital in 1880.

Western missionaries established the first modern hospitals, medical schools, universities, nurseries, orphanages and mental asylums across China.[2]

Many had left security, family and relative comfort to travel to the other side of the world. But in devoting their lives to the physical as well as the spiritual needs of others, they were following in a tradition going all the way back to the days of the early church.

The Christian Contribution to Healthcare and Hospitals

Because God has created all human beings in His image, with the capacity to reason, and a conscience, we expect to find a measure of medical advance in every civilisation. Greek, Roman, Indian and Islamic civilisations all produced great physicians and surgeons, but they did not create a culture of care (see chapter six).[3]

Little is known about the life of the Greek doctor **Hippocrates of Cos (c. 460-377 BC)**, but physicians in the 'Hippocratic tradition' promised that they would 'first do no harm' *(primum non nocere)*, they would not procure abortions, they would protect patients from exploitation, and they would respect patient confidentiality. The Christian ethic 'love your

---

2   William Huang, 'Forgotten Christians who gave China its best hospitals', *The Conservative Woman,* 26 March, 2020, https://conservativewoman.co.uk/forgotten-christians-who-gave-china-its-best-hospitals/ (accessed 7 April, 2020).

3   Vishal Mangalwadi, *The Book that Made your World* (Thomas Nelson, 2011), p. 301.

neighbour as yourself' (Lev. 19:18; Matt. 7:12; 22:39) and 'do not murder' (Exod. 20:13) was consistent with this tradition.

> The teaching of Jesus was the dynamic motivation behind the rise of hospitals, orphanages, leprosariums and hospices for the dying. For those who followed Jesus, the poor, the sick, the homeless, the prisoner, the unemployed, the stranger and the dying were the focus of the love of God and therefore of human care.[4]

The word 'hospital' comes from the Latin word *hospes*, or 'guest'. John Wyatt writes:

> A hospital is a place where we practice hospitality, neighbour-love to strangers, a bizarre concept first introduced by one Jesus of Nazareth.[5]

In Rome, the Christian noblewoman and scholar **Fabiola (d. 399)** established and funded a public hospital and cared herself for the sick and destitute. More Christian hospitals for the destitute and dying were founded by the reign of **Constantine (r. 306-337)**. They could be found from the Syrian and Byzantine East to the Western fringe of Christendom. The only previous 'hospitals' were the institutions used by the Roman army to restore soldiers to their fighting capacity. During the fourth century, the great city of Edessa (Urfa in modern Turkey) was ravaged by an outbreak of plague. The

---

4   Os Guinness, *Renaissance* (USA:IVP, 2014), p. 26.

5   John Wyatt, *Matters of Life and Death: Human Dilemmas in the light of the Christian Faith* (IVP, 2009), p. 248.

Christian deacon **Ephraim the Syrian (306-373)** founded hospitals to care for the victims.

Basil of Caesarea (330-379)[6] left family wealth and his legal career to embrace a monastic lifestyle. He saw *philanthropia* (active love for humankind) as an essential virtue. As Bishop of Caesarea, Basil founded a whole complex of hospitals, orphanages and hostels for the poor. He was always willing to provide practical care himself (he had attained some medical knowledge as a student):

> Even lepers, whose deformities and suppurations rendered them objects of particular revulsion, might be welcomed by the bishop with a kiss, and given both refuge and care. The more broken men and women were, the readier was Basil to glimpse Christ in them. The spectacle in a slave market of a boy sold by starving parents, the one child sacrificed that his siblings might have some scraps of food, provoked the bishop to a particularly scorching excoriation of the rich: 'The bread in your board belongs to the hungry; the cloak in your wardrobe to the naked; the shoes you let rot to the barefoot, the money in your vault to the destitute.'[7]

John Chrysostom (347-407), the bishop of Constantinople, used his influence to fund hospitals. Rich members of the laity were personally involved in care for the poor and sick. In

---

6   Mentioned also in chapter four, in relation to his opposition to abortion. Caesarea is now called Kayseri (in Turkey).

7   Tom Holland, *Dominion: The Making of the Western Mind* (Little, Brown, 2019), p. 124.

addition to medical care, these hospitals provided food for the hungry and cared for widows and orphans.[8]

Benedict of Nursia (c. 480-547) founded a monastic order. Care of the sick was one of the main duties, and a free infirmary was opened in Monte Cassino. The Benedictines:

> ... imprinted on Western consciousness the idea of humility and service as the true means of greatness. This idea became a defining feature of Western civilization. It is the opposite of the Asian idea that lesser beings must serve the greater.[9]

Monasteries not only displayed an ethic of care, they were committed to the preservation and propagation of learning (see chapter eight). God has provided us with 'two books'. First, the Bible. Second, natural revelation, that is creation and all we can learn from it. There is no need for a rigid division between theology and all the other disciplines. We learn of God and from God in all.

> Christ's followers preserved, transcribed and translated Greek medical manuscripts. Medieval Catholic monasteries absorbed Greek and Islamic medicine and enriched the tradition by accumulating knowledge, recording it in books, and carefully observing what treatment worked and what did not. Ancient philosophical, scientific and medical classics have come down to us substantially because monasteries had scriptoria where they copied books ... [10]

---

8   David Bentley Hart, *Atheist Delusions* (Yale University Press, 2010), pp. 30-1.

9   Vishal Mangalwadi, *The Book that Made your World*, p. 306.

10   Mangalwadi, p. 306.

Before the Islamic conquests of the seventh and eighth centuries, Christian churches could be found throughout the Middle East and North Africa. Christians established numerous free hospitals which were well served by physicians and surgeons. Some provided convalescent care. Some specialised in the care of the elderly. There were shelters for foundlings, the homeless and orphans. The Hospital of St John was built in Jerusalem in 1099: a complex of beautiful buildings well-equipped to care for around two thousand people. It also provided food and other help to the poor of the city. At Montpelier in 1145 the Hospital of the Holy Spirit was founded. It soon became a centre of medical training.

Hospitals were built by Christians throughout Western Europe during the Later Middle Ages. By the fourteenth century, England alone, with fewer than four million people, had six hundred hospitals; France, Germany and Italy had even more.[11] The Benedictines were responsible for more than two thousand hospitals, and in addition, by the mid-fifteenth century there were thirty-seven thousand Benedictine monasteries caring for the sick.[12]

The first modern book on surgery was written by the Catholic priest **Guy de Chauliac (1298-1368)**, who was educated at Montpelier and Bologna. His seven-volume work *Chirurgia Magna* included over three thousand references to other medical works, and would be translated into several languages, including English, French, Dutch, Italian, and

---

11 Alvin J. Schmidt, *How Christianity Changed the World* (Zondervan, 2004), p. 159.

12 Ibid., p. 157.

Provençal. It was widely used by physicians across Europe in the Later Middle Ages.[13]

During the sixteenth century, monastic networks offering care to the sick and needy were dissolved in those countries impacted by the Reformation. Peter Saunders, now the CEO of The International Christian Medical and Dental Association, suggests that Protestant clergy continued to demonstrate the Christian ethic of care:

> Clergy-physicians played an important role among Protestant ministers from the 16th through the 18th centuries. In an age in which trained physicians were especially uncommon in villages and rural areas, the Protestant belief in an educated clergy ensured a supply of persons who had both the leisure and the learning to read medical books. John Wesley (1703-1791) took a course in medicine so that as a minister he could be of help to those who had no regular physician. In 1746 he opened a dispensary and in the next year published a lay medical guide, 'Primitive Physick'.[14]

Thomas Sydenham (1624-1689) is remembered as 'The Father of English Medicine'. His *Observationes Medicae* ('Observations of Medicine') became the standard medical textbook for two centuries. His ethic of care focused on what treatment would be best for the individual patient. He

---

13   Roy Porter, *The Greatest Benefit to Mankind: A Medical History of Humanity from Antiquity to the Present* (HarperCollins, 1997), pp. 118-9.

14   Peter Saunders, 'Medicine and the Reformation', *Triple Helix,* Autumn 2017, Christian Medical Fellowship, https://www.cmf.org. uk/resources/publications/content/?context=article&id=26701 (accessed 16 April, 2020).

insisted on accurate observation and careful diagnosis: 'You must go to the bedside. It is there alone that you can learn disease'.[15] He used natural remedies where possible. During the Great Plague in 1665, he remained in London to treat those who were suffering, defying personal risk. Sydenham was motivated by a deep Christian faith. He summed up his approach when teaching medicine in his *Medical Observations concerning the History and Cure of Acute Diseases* (1668):

> Whoever applies himself to medicine should seriously weigh the following considerations:
>
> 1. He will one day have to render an account to the Supreme Judge of the lives of sick persons committed to his care.
>
> 2. Whatever skill or knowledge he may, by the divine favour, become possessed of, should be devoted above all things to the glory of God and the welfare of the human race.
>
> 3. He must remember that it is no mean or ignoble creature that he deals with. We may ascertain the worth of the human race since for its sake God's only begotten Son became man and thereby ennobled the nature that he took upon him.
>
> 4. The physician should bear in mind that he himself is not exempt from the common lot but is subject to the same laws of mortality and disease as his fellows and he will care for

---

15   Stephen Browne, 'Sydenham, The Physician', *Nucleus*, Spring 1996, Christian Medical Fellowship, https://www.cmf.org.uk/resources/publications/content/?context=article&id=529 (accessed 16 April, 2020).

the sick with more diligence and tenderness if he remembers that he himself is their fellow sufferer.[16]

During the eighteenth century, one of the practical out-workings of religious revival was the founding of a new generation of Christian hospitals supported mainly by voluntary subscriptions. Several leading hospitals were founded in London, including the Westminster (1719), Guy's (1724), St George's (1733), the Middlesex (1746), and Queen Charlotte's (1752). In addition, many of the older monastic hospitals were still open.

> When the National Health Service took over most voluntary hospitals, it became clear just how indebted the community was to these hospitals and the Christian zeal and money that supported them over centuries. In fact, the NHS was essentially created through the nationalisation of Christian hospitals like St Bartholomew's, St Thomas's, St Mary's and St George's.[17]

By the eighteenth century, Edinburgh was an internationally recognised medical centre. It had been deeply influenced by the Presbyterianism which had emerged from connections with Calvin's Geneva.[18]

For poor people who needed medical care outside of the hospital system, dispensaries were built, financed by charitable donations. Many churches would preach an annual sermon on

---

16   Ibid.

17   Saunders, 'Medicine and the Reformation'.

18   Ibid.

the theme of compassion for the sick and poor, and take up offerings for the local dispensary afterwards.

Compassion for the Mentally Ill

The Christian ethic of compassion extended beyond those with physical illness or material want. During the Early Middle Ages the mentally disturbed were cared for in monasteries, and later on separate facilities were provided. But treatment could be harsh, and the assumption that insanity could be associated with criminality sometimes led to punitive regimes.

It was the Christian conviction that all should be treated with dignity that impelled reformers such as French physician, **Phillipe Pinel (1745-1826)**[19], Quaker philanthropist **William Tuke (1732-1822)**,[20] American campaigner **Dorothea Dix (1802-1887)**,[21] English social campaigner **Lord Shaftesbury (1801-1885)**,[22] and many others to take a lead, both in practical care and political reforms to safeguard the interests of the mentally ill.[23] The 1845 Reform Act pushed through by Shaftesbury has been described as 'the Magna Carta of the liberation of the insane'.[24]

---

19 Schmidt, p. 161.

20 'William Tuke', BBC History, https://www.bbc.co.uk/history/historic_figures/tuke_william.shtml (accessed 16 April, 2020).

21 Schmidt, p. 162.

22 Richard Turnbull, *Shaftesbury The Great Reformer* (Lion, 2009), chapter 5, 'Shaftesbury and Mental Health', pp. 58-73.

23 Kathleen Heasman, *Evangelicals in Action: An Appraisal of their Social Work* (Geoffry Bles, 1962), chapter XII, 'The Unsound in Mind and Body', pp. 208-24.

24 Ibid., p. 209.

Christian Nursing

Nursing worldwide has been pioneered by Christian voluntary efforts. During the period of the early church, widows and deaconesses cared for the sick. During the Middle Ages, monks and nuns provided nursing care (see also chapter six).

Modern nursing dates back to the pioneering practice of an order of Lutheran deaconesses at Kaiserswerth in Northern Germany. This began when **Pastor Theodor Fleidner (1800-1864)** gave refuge to a sick and destitute ex-prisoner and provided nursing care. He then established a hospital with a hundred beds, and trained poor women as nurses. By 1894 nearly eight thousand deaconesses were serving in Germany, in hospitals, orphanages and schools and as parish helpers.[25]

When the young English aristocrat **Florence Nightingale (1820-1910)** visited Kaiserswerth, she was inspired to defy her horrified parents and devote her life to nursing. Famously, she transformed the vile conditions in the British military hospital in the Crimea during the Crimean War (1853-1856). She spent the next fifty years developing and promoting modern nursing. She regarded excellent nursing as both an art and a science, but all motivated with the Christian conviction that each patient has dignity:

> Nursing is an art ... it requires an exclusive devotion as hard a preparation as any painter's or sculptor's work; for what is the having to do with dead canvass or dead marble, compared

---

25   Kenneth S. Latourette, *A History of Christianity,* vol. II (Harper & Son, 1975), p. 1136.

with having to do with the living body, the temple of God's spirit? (Florence Nightingale)[26]

Few today have heard of **Andrew Reed (1787-1862)**. He was a great pioneer in care for orphans, those with learning disabilities and the terminally ill. Reed came from a humble background, left school early, and trained to work as a watchmaker. He was converted at the age of fifteen. Four years later he began ministerial training at a small nonconformist college. Reed took up the pastorate of New Road Chapel, London when he was twenty-four, and served faithfully there for fifty years. During his ministry the church grew from sixty to two thousand members. It was situated in a poor area, surrounded by pitiful scenes of squalor and destitution. Life expectancy was short. Many infants were left orphaned with no-one to care for them. Before he married, Andrew lived with his sister Martha. They took destitute orphans into their own home, but soon Andrew raised funds for a large home to accommodate orphans.[27]

After Andrew married, his wife Elizabeth worked alongside Martha in charitable ministries. Meanwhile Andrew juggled pastoral responsibilities and preaching with fundraising and oversight of the orphanages. He became increasingly disturbed at the lack of provision for children with learning disabilities. Asylums, hospitals, and workhouses had sections

26 Quoted in Stephen Fouch, 'Care and Compassion', CMF Files No. 50, Spring 2013, https://www.cmf.org.uk/resources/publications/content/?context=article&id=26045 (accessed 17 April, 2020).

27 Ian J. Shaw, *The Greatest is Charity: The Life of Andrew Reed, preacher and philanthropist* (Evangelical Press, 2005).

for those labelled as 'lunatics' where all those born with learning difficulties and those suffering mental illness were put together indiscriminately. They were often appallingly treated. Reed travelled through Europe to find out how such children were cared for in a number of pioneering institutions run by Christians.

In 1848, Reed opened a home in Highgate for children with learning difficulties: the first in Britain. He then raised funds to purchase the Earlswood Estate, near Redhill, Surrey. Prince Albert laid the foundation stone in 1853. This was transformed by voluntary gifts into The Royal Earlswood Hospital which could house up to five hundred children. It became internationally known for the enlightened way in which children with severe learning difficulties were treated.

Reed also became a pioneer in the care of the terminally ill. Pastoring a church in a very poor area, he saw hospitals discharging patients who were 'incurable' who might end up on the streets, or in the workhouse. Reed opened a home in Carshalton in 1855, which looked after about forty people. This was replaced by a larger hospital and home for terminally ill patients at Putney (now the Royal Hospital for Neuro-Disability).

Others followed this lead, and a host of other initiatives to help the terminally ill followed. To bring Reed's story up to date: **Cicely Saunders (1918-2005)** opened St Christopher's Hospice in 1967, widely considered the first modern hospice. Like Andrew Reed, Cicely Saunders was motivated by her deep Christian commitment. The hospice movement, and its commitment to palliative care, has spread to many countries.

Dr John Wyatt explains the Christian ethos lying behind the best palliative care. Respect for life and the interests of the patient are central. A good doctor acknowledges when 'treatment that is excessively burdensome, relative to its benefits, should be withdrawn'.[28] But while a doctor may decide that a treatment is futile, they can *never* decide that a life is futile. If invasive life-support is ended, the intent must never be to kill. Many Christians today provide and promote excellent palliative care (and they oppose moves to legalise euthanasia or assisted suicide).

> Specialists say that, with appropriate expertise, pain can be completely abolished or dramatically ameliorated in over 95% of cases. In fact, physical pain in terminal illness is rarely a major problem for carers these days. The problem pain is spiritual pain, emotional pain, relational pain.[29]

Christian hospices have developed ways of using the skills of medics and nurses, as well as chaplains and carers, 'to treat the whole person in response to the "total pain" of dying'.[30]

Healthcare is now regarded as the obligation of the State, but Christian voluntary contributions laid the foundation. Researcher James Bartholomew has spent years studying the Welfare State. He documents that before the National Health Service was founded in 1948, Britain had one of the leading

---

28 John Wyatt, *Matters of Life and Death* (IVP/CMF, 2009), p. 223.
29 Ibid., p. 230.
30 Ibid.

medical services in the world, and much of it was due to Christian charitable giving and input.[31]

Christian Mission and Healthcare

Worldwide, Christian missionaries have led the way in providing medical clinics, blood banks, mental health programmes, and alcohol and drug rehabilitation.[32] Working in some of the toughest situations on earth has led to some major medical breakthroughs, such as the missionary Paul Brand's pioneering treatment of leprosy, which has been internationally recognised.[33]

Christian missionaries have also been at the forefront of providing medical care for women. In 1892 a young American woman, **Ida Scudder (1870-1960)**, visited her missionary parents in South India. She had just graduated from college in America, and was determined to return there. She was eagerly anticipating enjoying the greater material comforts the United States could offer.

But one fateful evening she received three separate calls for help. Two Hindus (one Brahmin and one from the Mudaliar caste), and a Muslim all begged Ida to attend their wives, each struggling in labour. Ida explained that she had no medical qualifications. Her father, an experienced doctor, should

---

31 James Bartholomew, *The Welfare State We're In,* pp. 87-150.

32 *Christianity and Freedom* (CUP, 2016), vol. 2, pp. 4, 92; Ruth Tucker, *From Jerusalem to Irian Jaya: A Biographical History of Christian Missions* (Zondervan, 2004), chapter 12, 'Medical Missions', pp. 327-47.

33 Philip Yancey, 'Paul Brand', in *Heroes: Five Remarkable Christians* (IVP, 1991), pp. 7-28.

attend the births. Each man explained, 'I can't take a man to see my wife!' The next morning Ida was horrified to learn that all three women had died in childbirth during the night.

Her life plan changed dramatically. She trained as a doctor in America and returned to India. In 1900 she established what would become Vellore Christian Medical College, designed to train Indian female doctors.

> She brought new hope and dignity to women in South India, giving them the benefits of modern medicine previously denied them by cultural barriers. She opened up the health care professions to women from all faiths and backgrounds, encouraging families to allow their daughters to train as nurses and doctors and showing by her own example and her students' achievements that women could equal men both in medical studies and clinical proficiency, and excel in leadership even in the toughest of times. Ida Scudder inspired hundreds of young medical professionals to take the words of Jesus as their motto. He said that he had come, 'not to be served but to serve.' [34]

Mahatma Gandhi described Vellore Christian Medical College as the best medical college in Asia.[35] Today it is one of the top-ranked educational, healthcare and research institutes

---

34 'Dr Ida Sophia Scudder', https://www.cmch-vellore.edu/SinglePage.aspx?pid=P171127016&mid=M171211128 (accessed 16 April, 2020).

35 Mangalwadi, p. 311.

in India, with a network of teaching hospitals spread across six campuses.[36]

Robert Woodberry spent years researching the impact of Bible-believing missionaries around the world. He found that:

> Missionaries ... typically opened the first hospitals and clinics, and pioneered Western medical education around the world. Informally, many missionaries also taught hygiene and rudimentary medical knowledge and introduced new crops and livestock that improved the quality of local diets. Thus, the historical prevalence of Protestant missionaries is associated with longer life expectancies and lower infant mortality rates.[37]

How do we explain this? Rosie Knowles, a GP in Sheffield, testifies:

> Christianity gives men and women a new perspective and allegiance; their lives are spent in joyful, grateful service of the God who has redeemed them. In many ways, Christianity and medicine are natural allies; medicine offers people unique opportunities to express their faith in practical caring for others, embodying the command of Christ: 'whatever

---

36 'The Christian Medical College, Vellore: Our Story', https://www. cmch-vellore.edu/content.aspx?Pid=P171127016 (accessed 16 April, 2020).

37 Robert Woodberry, 'Protestant Missionaries and the Centrality of Conversion Attempts for the Spread of Education, Printing, Colonial Reform and Political Democracy', in *Christianity and Freedom,* vol. 1 (CUP, 2016), p. 385.

you did for one of the least of these brothers of mine, you did for me'. (Matt. 25:40)[38]

Further Reading

Alvin J. Schmidt, *How Christianity Changed the World* (Zondervan, 2004), pp. 151-67.

John Wyatt, *Matters of Life and Death* (IVP/CMF, 2009), pp. 239-63.

---

38 Rosie Knowles, 'The Christian contribution to healthcare', Christian Medical Fellowship, *Nucleus,* Freshers Edition, 2020, https://www.cmf.org.uk/resources/publications/content/?context =article&id=26520 (accessed 20 April, 2020).

8 Education for All

I first discovered the Bible as a student in India. It transformed
me as an individual.[1]

The Indian scholar Vishal Mangalwadi (b. 1949) converted
to Christianity when he investigated the Christian holy book
and realised that the thread running throughout is God's
desire to bless all nations. He went on to study the impact of
the Bible on his own nation, and concluded:

> My investigation of whether God had truly blessed India
> through the Bible yielded incredible discoveries: the
> university where I was studying, the municipality and
> democracy I lived in, the High Court behind my house
> and the legal system it represented, the modern Hindi that
> I spoke as my mother tongue, the secular newspaper for
> which I had begun to write ... the botanical garden to the
> east, the public library near our garden, the railway lines that
> intersected in my city, the medical system I depended on, the

---

1   Vishal Mangalwadi, *The Book that Made Your World* (Thomas Nelson,
     2011), p. 23.

Agricultural Institute across town—all of these came to my city because some people took the Bible seriously ... We were always told that India's freedom was a result of Mahatma Gandhi's struggle; it was a surprise to learn that, in reality, India's freedom was a fruit of the Bible. Before the Bible, our people did not even have the modern notions of nation or freedom.[2]

As Mangalwadi went on to investigate the impact of the Bible on nations beyond his own, he realised that:

The Bible created the modern world of science and learning because it gave us the Creator's vision of what reality is all about.[3]

We Are Able to Study Because the Cosmos Is Ordered

The heavens declare the glory of God, the skies proclaim the work of his hands. (Ps. 19:1)

Heaven and earth are full of your glory! (Isa. 6:3)

The cosmos can be investigated, discovered and explored, because it is created by God, who is Himself characterised by order, truth, reason, beauty, love and justice. God has placed us in a world designed to be a dazzling theatre of His glory,[4] filled with an astonishing array of natural resources to be developed.

---

2   Ibid., pp. 55-6.

3   Ibid., p. xxi.

4   John Calvin, *Institutes of the Christian Religion*, Book 1 *The Knowledge of God the Creator*, Section 8, J. T. McNeill., (ed), F. L.Battles (trans)

We Are Able to Study Because We Are Created in the Image of the Triune God

The Creator has given us the God-like capacity to develop earth's resources by means of reason, creativity, intelligence, and hard work. God has given all human beings the divine mandate to manage the natural world.

> So God created mankind in his own image,
>   in the image of God he created him;
>   male and female he created them.
> God blessed them and said to them, 'Be fruitful and
> increase in number; fill the earth and subdue it. Rule over
> the fish in the sea and the birds in the sky and over every
> living creature that moves on the ground.' (Gen. 1:27-8)

The biblical terms 'subdue' and 'rule over' (sometimes translated exercise 'dominion'), mean that we are to steward and manage the earth on behalf of the great King. To do that we need to study and understand the creation.

We are created beings, but we are not 'mere' creatures, like the animals. Uniquely among creatures, we are created in the image of the Creator, so we are *creative* beings. We are able to reason, observe, experiment, deduce, speak, infer, argue, communicate, love and relate *because* God created us in His image.

In order to be able to fulfil our potential as creative beings, we have to learn of God and of His creation. And because God has endowed every human being with the capacity to reason, that capacity should be developed. Every child's unique gifts

---

(Westminster Press, 2 volumes, 1960), Vol. 1. p. 61.

and capacities should be nurtured and developed. Every adult should go on learning throughout life, developing the mind that God has given us.

Supremely we are created to know God. We learn of God through His Word. All people, in every place, need to be able to read the Bible, and have access to the Bible in their own language. That is why Christians have been at the forefront of literacy provision worldwide.

Christian Commitment to Education

> Great are the works of the Lord, studied by all who delight in them. (Ps. 111:2)

This verse was inscribed in Latin over the archway to the main scientific laboratory in Cambridge for many years. It is now inscribed in English over the door of the new Cavendish Laboratory, home to the Cambridge Physics department. Science represents our effort to understand God's handiwork. The Bible teaches that a rational being created and sustains the natural world. Human beings, as rational beings, can, in turn, discover the laws of nature, and then act on nature, effectively and rationally.

This was the key to many intellectual undertakings, among them the rise of science.

The Bible places high premium on knowledge. But this doesn't come by means of mystical experience or mere devotion and meditation. It comes from study and hard work, investigating the natural world, and building on the work of others. That's why we need education. Historically, Christians have been passionately committed to education for all, and in many countries they have been the first to provide schools, colleges and universities.

Jesus Christ told His followers to go make disciples of all nations, *teaching* them to obey all that He had commanded. The early church took this seriously. Converts were carefully instructed in doctrine. Often over two to three years, before baptism, they would be instructed using manuals and catechisms. New converts, both men and women, were often taught both the Scriptures and a useful trade. Instructing women as well as men was revolutionary. Such teaching often continued after baptism. Soon catechetical schools were established. They taught Christian doctrine, but increasingly mathematics and medicine as well.[5] By the fourth century, **Augustine of Hippo (354-430)** said that Christian women were better informed in divine matters than pagan male philosophers.[6]

Augustine himself, a North African bishop, reflected deeply on the fact that all humans are created in the image of God. Whether or not they are Christians, they are not only rational but also truth-seeking. He wrote:

> Has not the genius of man invented and applied countless astonishing arts, partly the result of necessity, partly the result of exuberant invention, so that this vigour of mind ... betokens an inexhaustible wealth in the human nature which can invent, learn, or employ such arts. What wonderful –

---

5   Alvin J. Schmidt, *How Christianity Changed the World* (Zondervan, 2004), p. 172.

6   Ibid.

one might say stupefying – advances has human industry made in the arts of weaving and building, or agriculture and navigation! ... what skill has been attained in measures and numbers! With what sagacity have the movements and connections of the stars been discovered![7]

And what made all this possible? Augustine was certain. It was all because of:

the unspeakable blessing that God has conferred upon his creation – a rational nature.[8]

Augustine believed that Christians can and should learn from all the learning known to pagan philosophers, so they should be taught languages, history, grammar, logic and sciences. He wrote a comprehensive text book of all the various branches of learning to date which became the standard text for European universities through the Middle Ages.[9] He used his mighty intellect to formulate theology, philosophy and other fields of study, and the impact has echoed down through the centuries. For example, his six-volume work *On Music* built a philosophy of music from biblical, scientific and philosophical foundations (including Greek thought). God placed in us the capacity and ability to praise Him in song and instrumental music. Augustine laid out a theology of music, and showed that God providentially ordained the rational, eternal, unchangeable and objective principles behind it. The scientific basis of music lies in mathematical patterns embedded in the core of

7   Quoted in Rodney Stark, *Victory of Reason*, pp. 9-10.

8   Ibid.

9   Mangalwadi, p. 208.

creation. Our Creator 'encoded music into the structure of the universe'.[10]

Music that can be appreciated by human senses is only the footprint of the divine music of the universe.[11]

As the Western Roman world disintegrated, Christian monasteries preserved the literary remains of ancient Rome. In the East, it was a Christian civilisation that united the intellectual cultures of the Greek, Egyptian and Syrian worlds, and that preserved Hellenic wisdom in academies and libraries in Greece, Syria, and Asia Minor.

The great medieval philosopher and theologian **Thomas Aquinas (1225-1274)** was certain that Christians can learn from unbelievers because the rational Creator God has placed His natural law on their hearts. All truth is God's truth. We can be confident as we study that God's general revelation (nature) never contradicts and always harmonises with His special revelation (Scripture).

Universities: Their Christian Foundation

As Christian monasteries and cathedral schools developed into the earliest universities they were not just preserving and passing on the knowledge of the past. Communities of scholars gathered to study and push forward the pursuit of

---

10 Ibid., p. 12.

11 Junxiao Bai, 'The Spectrum of the Divine Order: Goodness, Beauty, and Harmony', *Soundings: An Interdisciplinary Journal*, Volume 102, Number 1, 2019, pp.1-30, p. 5, https://muse.jhu.edu/article/715037/pdf (accessed 21 April, 2020).

knowledge. They were willing to critique the ancients.[12] The first universities were founded in Bologna (1088), Paris (late eleventh century), Oxford and Cambridge (both around 1200). These were not just small groups of scholars. By the early thirteenth century Paris, Bologna, Oxford and Toulouse each had between a thousand and fifteen hundred students. By the early fifteenth century almost every state in Europe had a university. There were nearly sixty in total, stretching from St Andrews (1412) and Rostock (1419) in the North, to Catania (1444) and Seville (1254) in the South; from Cracow (1364) in the East, to Lisbon (1290) in the West. These universities had generous financial endowments. They encouraged a significant measure of free enquiry and debate. Because of a common language, Latin, the universities in the different European countries were integrated, and scholars moved freely between them.[13]

It is untrue that Christianity suppressed scientific endeavour. After the 'Enlightenment' the idea took hold that Christianity plunged Europe into the 'Dark Ages'. In fact, so much technical progress took place during these centuries that by 1200 European technology surpassed anything in the world. Mediaeval Europe also excelled in philosophy and science.[14]

---

12 Rodney Stark, *For the Glory of God: How Monotheism led to Reformations, Science, Witch-hunts and the End of Slavery* (Princeton University Press, 2003), pp. 140-1; 143-6.

13 David Bentley Hart, *Atheist Delusions* (Yale University Press, 2010), p. 71; Rodney Stark, *For the Glory of God*, p. 141.

14 Stark, p. 134.

Generations of school children were told, wrongly, that the Catholic Church thought the earth was flat, and so opposed Christopher Columbus's voyage of exploration in 1492. But for centuries before, it had been accepted that the earth was round. The Venerable Bede (673-735) taught that the earth was round. So did Thomas Aquinas (1225-1274). The most popular medieval textbook on astronomy, by John of Sacrobosco (1200-1256), taught that all heavenly bodies, including the earth, were spherical.[15]

Christian theology was fundamental to the rise of modern science. The leading scientific figures in the sixteenth and seventeenth centuries were overwhelmingly devout Christians 'who believed it their duty to comprehend God's handiwork'.[16]

The reformed theologian **John Calvin (1509-1564)** was clear about the terrible effects of sin, but he was equally clear that in common (or everyday) grace God has endowed all human beings with reason. He taught that we should be humble and willing to admire and learn from the wisdom of the past, and that all branches of learning, including science, are God's gift. We dishonour the Spirit of God if we neglect them:

> Whenever we come upon these matters in secular writers, let this admirable light of truth shining in them teach us that the mind of men, though fallen and perverted from its wholeness, is nevertheless clothed and ornamented with God's excellent gifts. If we regard the Spirit of God as the sole fountain of truth, we shall neither reject the truth itself,

15   Ibid., p. 123.
16   Ibid., pp. 123; 198-9.

nor despise it wherever it shall appear, unless we wish to dishonour the Spirit of God.[17]

To those who argued that we cannot learn from unbelievers, Calvin replied that the Holy Spirit works sanctification only in true believers. But the same Spirit gives a measure of light and ability to unbelievers, and we can learn from them in some fields:

> What then? Shall we deny that the truth shone upon the ancient jurists who established civic order and discipline with such great equity? Shall we say that the philosophers were blind in their fine observation and artful description of nature? Shall we say that those men were devoid of understanding who conceived the art of disputation and taught us to speak reasonably? Shall we say that they are insane who developed medicine, devoting their labour to our benefit? What shall we say of all the mathematical sciences? Shall we consider them the ravings of madmen? No, we cannot read the writings of the ancients on these subjects without great admiration ... But shall we count anything praiseworthy or noble without recognising at the same time that it comes from God? ... if the Lord has willed that we be helped in physics, dialectic, mathematics, and other like disciplines, by the work and ministry of the ungodly, let us use this assistance. For if we neglect God's gift freely offered in these arts, we ought to suffer just punishment for our sloth.[18]

---

17   Calvin, pp. 273-4.

18   Ibid., pp. 274-5.

The Puritans also believed that it is a Christian's duty to study and understand God's handiwork, as that brings Him glory. Puritan intellectuals defined science as a religious calling. During the early years of the Royal Society of London, membership was dominated by Puritans.[19]

Science still attracts many Christians to study at the highest levels. In the mid-twentieth century a survey of more than 60,000 university professors in America found that the majority of those involved in the 'hard sciences' professed to be religious; unbelief was far more prevalent in the social sciences.[20] There are many committed Christians deeply involved in the scientific endeavour. And there are a significant number of scientists, whether Christian or not, who reject a purely materialistic explanation of the universe and the origins of life. For example, the Discovery Institute's Center for Science and Culture in the United States sponsors scientific research in a variety of fields. It affirms that human beings and nature are the result of intelligent design, rather than a blind and undirected process.[21]

Schools: The Christian Contribution

For many centuries teaching children was seen as the job of the Church. The oldest still-functioning school in Britain is King's School, Canterbury, established by Augustine of Canterbury in 597. During the Middle Ages, the Church

---

19   Stark, pp. 158-9.

20   Ibid., pp. 194-5.

21   The Discovery Institute, https://www.discovery.org/id/about/ (accessed 22 April, 2020).

continued to provide education. But it was after the Reformation that universal literacy was seen as essential so that everyone could read the Scriptures for themselves. The 'desire to read the Bible became the fuel that drove the engine of Europe's literacy'.[22] The Reformer Martin Luther believed that it was a crime for parents not to ensure the education of their children. During the Reformation in Europe, there was a surge in the building of girls' schools in Protestant areas. Anna Maria Van Schurman (1607-1678) was a skilled linguist, with knowledge of thirteen languages. Brought up in the Dutch Reformed Church, in 1638 she published a treatise on the need for women to be educated. *'Ignorance is not fitting for a Christian woman'*, she wrote.[23]

Areas with the earliest mass literacy were those areas impacted by the Reformation: the Protestant areas of Switzerland and Germany, the Netherlands, Scandinavia, Iceland, lowland Scotland, the Faroe Islands, Puritan areas of England, and the early American colonies.[24]

A famous protestant educationalist was **John Comenius (1592-1670)** of Moravia.[25] He started schools for poor girls

---

22 Mangalwadi, p. 213.

23 S. O. Becker and L. Wößmann, 'Luther and the Girls: Religious Denomination and the Female Education Gap in 19th Century Prussia', *IZA Discussion Paper* No. 3837, November 2008, http://ftp.iza.org/dp3837.pdf (accessed 11 August, 2018).

24 Robert Woodberry, 'Protestant Missionaries and the Centrality of Conversion Attempts for the Spread of Education, Printing, Colonial Reform and Political Democracy', in *Christianity and Freedom*, vol. 1 (Cambridge University Press, 2016), pp. 367-90, p. 373.

25 An area in the present day Czech Republic.

and boys because he wanted everyone made in God's image to learn of God, man and nature. Because of his reformed convictions, he spent much of his life as a religious refugee. He still managed to write around ninety books on education. His advice was sought at the highest level in England, Sweden, the Netherlands and Austria.

Comenius believed that education should be a happy experience for children, that all learning should be carefully adapted to the stage of development of each child, and that children should learn by inquiry. In 1658 he published *The World of Things Obvious to the Senses drawn in Pictures*.[26] Many believe this to be the first children's picture book. It started with several pages of pictures of animals, then pictures showing everyday activities like tending gardens and brewing beer. The book went on to cover theology, anatomy, biology and astronomy. It aimed to teach about the whole world *via* the senses. This visual approach was a breakthrough, so was Comenius' decision to publish both a German (i.e. vernacular) edition as well as a Latin edition. At one point it was the most used textbook in Europe for elementary education, and was translated into most European and some of the Oriental languages.

Isaac Watts (1675-1748) is best known as a hymn writer ('Jesus shall reign where'er the sun'; 'Joy to the World'; 'Alas, and did my Saviour bleed', 'Our God our help in ages past'; and 'When I survey the wondrous cross' are some of his best

---

26 https://publicdomainreview.org/2014/05/14/in-the-image-of-god-john-comenius-and-the-first-childrens-picture-book/ (accessed 11 December, 2019).

known hymns). He was also a gifted pastor and preacher. Few today realise that he also wrote textbooks on a range of subjects – language, logic, mathematics, science – which were used in Britain and internationally up to university level.

Isaac Watts spent several years as a tutor. He was passionate about the importance of teaching children well from the earliest age. He regarded teaching as one of the noblest occupations.

> How lovely it is to see a teacher waiting upon those that are slow of understanding, and taking due time and pains to make the learner understand what he means without upbraiding him with his weakness.[27]

Watts' textbook on educating children, entitled *A Discourse on the Education of Children and Youth* was enormously popular. Because God has given everyone a rational nature and a soul that will never die, he stressed the need to give girls as well as boys an excellent education. He believed that teachers don't just convey information: they teach by the way that they live. Teachers must be kind and teach children to be kind. Teachers must be cheerful and encourage children to be cheerful. They must avoid being boring: they should use visual aids, diagrams, maps and different colours. Lessons must be based on observation, not just instruction. Youngsters must be encouraged to be curious and to think for themselves, and to think clearly and logically. They should be taken out on trips. As much travel as possible should be encouraged. They should

---

27   David G. Fountain, *Isaac Watts Remembered* (Gospel Standard Trust, 1974), pp. 36-7.

be trained to be diligent and to read widely. Above all they are to be pointed to their Creator. Knowing God brings joy, so teachers must demonstrate that joy. As one of Watts' hymns states:

Religion never was designed to make our pleasures less.[28]

Watts' best-selling work was *Divine Songs attempted in Easy Language for the Use of Children* published in 1715. It went through over a thousand editions, and sold more than seven million copies in various countries (the population of Britain in Watts' lifetime was about six million). One of the most well-known poems for children was entitled 'Against Idleness and Mischief' with the opening lines:

How doth the little busy bee improve the shining hour!

This was so universally known by children in the nineteenth century that Lewis Carroll was famously able to parody it in *Alice in Wonderland*, knowing that *everyone* would recognise the allusion.[29]

Isaac Watts' work on the *Improvement of the Mind* was also very popular. This was a textbook on how to increase in

---

28 Isaac Watts, 'Come we that love the Lord and let our joys be known'.

29 Isaac Watts, 'How doth the little busy bee, Improve each shining hour, And gather honey all the day, From every opening flower! In works of labor or of skill, I would be busy too; For Satan finds some mischief still, For idle hands to do.' Famously parodied by Lewis Carroll in *Alice in Wonderland*: 'How doth the little crocodile, Improve his shining tail, And pour the waters of the Nile, On every golden scale! How cheerfully he seems to grin, How neatly spreads his claws, And welcomes little fishes in, With gently smiling jaws!'

wisdom, godliness and usefulness throughout life.[30] It contains practical instructions on study skills, wise reading, useful conversation and ways to make social occasions edifying.

During the eighteenth century, those who could not, in conscience, conform to the rites and ceremonies of the Established Church (dissenters) were not allowed to go to English universities. They developed their own academies which played a significant role in educational provision. Isaac Watts' textbooks were hugely popular in these academies. Many eighteenth-century dissenters had a voracious thirst for learning. Many of those who had to leave school at an early age applied themselves diligently to education in their spare time, learning Latin, Greek, Hebrew and other languages. William Carey, for example, came from a pitifully poor background but taught himself Latin at age twelve, and later mastered Greek, Hebrew, French and Dutch. As a missionary in India he learned dozens of languages and dialects.

During the eighteenth and nineteenth centuries, the voluntary efforts of Christians led to an extraordinary expansion of education for children, including the very poorest. One well-known pioneer was **Robert Raikes (1735-1811)**. He was the crusading editor of the *Gloucester Journal*. Shocked at the conditions in the local prison, he became convinced that 'vice could be better prevented than cured'. Education would be the best prevention. He discussed this with a neighbouring vicar, and they came up with idea of

---

30 Isaac Watts, *Improvement of the Mind*, http://richelibreetheureux. com/wp-content/uploads/pdf/improvementofmin00wattuoft.pdf (accessed 22 April, 2020).

schools that could be run by volunteers on Sundays. This was the only day that poor children would be able to attend (they were sent out to work on the other six days). The teaching would include basic literacy.

One Sunday afternoon, in July 1780, a Christian woman called Mrs Meredith welcomed poor children into her home in Sooty Alley Gloucester. The first Sunday school! The idea took off. By 1831 about a quarter of England's 1.25 million children were attending Sunday schools. This depended on the voluntary efforts of tens of thousands of Christians.

Another pioneer of education for all was **Hannah More (1745-1833)**. She was a successful writer whose works at one time outsold Jane Austen's by ten to one. One of the stars on the London social scene, she was converted through reading a book by the evangelical John Newton (author of 'Amazing Grace'). After her conversion she poured her writing ability into the cause of the gospel and doing good to the poor.

Modern feminists celebrate **Mary Wollstonecraft (1759-1797)**, who argued that women should receive education like men. They rarely mention Hannah More, who also, like Wollstonecraft, wanted to see girls educated. Hannah More wrote the best-selling *Strictures on the Modern System of Female Education* in 1799.[31] Unlike Wollstonecraft, she also put words into action. After her conversion to evangelical Christianity Hannah More gave sacrificially of her own time and resources to establish schools for poor girls as well as boys.

---

31 Hannah More, *Strictures on the Modern System of Female Education*, 1799, https://quod.lib.umich.edu/e/ecco/004902140.0001.001/1:6.1? rgn=div2;view=fulltext (accessed 22 April, 2020)

She established schools for the poor against strong opposition. Her *Common Repository Tracts* (cheaply produced booklets with interesting stories illustrated with vivid engravings) sold widely. They promoted positive family values, as well as the avoidance of drunkenness, violence and debt. Her life and writings resulted in great social good. Many believe that her influence helped avert violent revolution at a time when many feared a re-run of the French Revolution.

During the nineteenth century the work of schools founded and run by Christians had a significant impact. Some children in the rapidly growing towns and cities were so destitute that they felt ashamed to go to Sunday school. Many Christians responded by opening 'Ragged Schools' which not only gave free teaching, but food and clothes as well. These were staffed by thousands of Christian volunteers. One of the pioneers of these schools was a Christian called **John Pounds (1766-1839)**, known as the crippled cobbler of Portsmouth. He taught children reading, writing, arithmetic, as well as skills such as carpentry, cooking and shoe-making. Other schools were set up on what was called the Lancaster-Bell or monitorial principle, where older pupils helped to teach the younger ones.

Many Christians met the needs that faced them in their own communities. During the 1840s for example, Richard Dawes became vicar of King's Somborne in Hampshire. Finding that there was no school in this village, he used £500 of his own funds to start one. He ran it himself, and taught a hundred and fifty-eight pupils. Like John Comenius and Isaac Watts, Richard Dawes wanted to make education pleasurable and relevant. He emphasised nature observation, using experiments, and taking the children out on trips.[32]

Largely because of the huge and often voluntary devotion to education of so many Christian people in Britain, most of the British working class achieved a basic level of literacy. This was remarkable, given the long working hours for children as well as parents. Researcher James Bartholomew has estimated that school attendance may have been higher before it was made compulsory in 1870 than it is now (given current truancy levels). The incredible levels of committed and often voluntary contributions by Christians led to equally incredible literacy rates. Surveys of coalminers, seamen and marines in England between 1840 and 1865 indicate that between eighty and ninety per cent of adults could read, and that proportion was rising rapidly.[33] By contrast, the Department for Education and Skills found in 2006 that one in five adults in Britain were thought to be 'functionally illiterate'.[34]

Education and Mission

Turning to the international perspective:

> Western missions ... birthed, financed, and nurtured hundreds of universities, thousands of colleges and tens

---

32 James Bartholomew, *The Welfare State We're In* (Politico's, 2006), pp. 154-6.

33 'Functional Illiteracy' was not being able to find a plumber in the yellow pages, or not being able to see where a pop group is giving a concert though it is written on a simple poster, Bartholomew, p. 159.

34 Bartholomew, pp. 167-8.

of thousands of schools. They educated millions and transformed nations.[35]

The reason behind this is that Protestants wanted people to be able to read the Bible for themselves, and in their own language. Wherever Protestant missionaries went, they developed written forms of spoken languages; created fonts, introduced printing, and printed the first newspapers and textbooks, as well as Bibles. They pioneered schools as they aimed for mass literacy.[36]

Two examples of missionaries committed to educational provision are Ann Judson, missionary to Burma, and William Carey, missionary to India, both of whom have been mentioned already (see chapters 4 and 5). Ann Judson (1789-1826) was one of the first overseas missionaries from America. Following her conversion at around the age of sixteen in 1805, she soon started teaching in school as she had great desire to impart the knowledge of God and His world to others. Aged twenty-one, she and her husband Adoniram left family, friends and all they knew in New England and started a Christian mission in Burma. Ann started schools for girls. She was only one of many Christians to promote female education in cultures where it was strictly forbidden.[37]

William Carey (1761-1834) came from a pitifully poor background, but educated himself while making a living as a cobbler. He tirelessly researched the situation for the gospel in

---

35 Mangalwadi, *The Book that Made your World*, pp. 207-8.

36 Woodberry, pp. 367-90, p. 373.

37 Sharon James, *Ann Judson* (Evangelical Press, 2015).

every country, and was convinced that the Great Commission was applicable for Christians in his day. When this humble Baptist preacher and his young wife left for India in 1793 many thought he was insane. But Carey would prove the gainsayers wrong, and today he is often remembered as the 'Father of missions'. In the face of often seemingly impossible difficulties, he persevered. 'I can plod,' he famously commented. But he also had faith that God could work through his humble efforts, and do the impossible. His motto was:

Expect great things from God; attempt great things for God

Carey translated the Scriptures into many Indian languages, trained Indian ministers, promoted social reforms, began dozens of schools for Indian children of all castes, pioneered lending libraries, published the first books on science and natural history in India, pioneered the printing industry in India, and became Professor of Bengali, Sanskrit and Marathi at Fort William College in Calcutta. He translated and printed great Indian religious classics, transformed Bengali into the foremost literary language of India, and established the first newspaper printed in any Asian language.[38]

Christians in India still play a leading role in promoting education for those regarded as 'untouchable', but they sometimes still run up against traditional resistance. 'In the

---

38 Vishal and Ruth Mangalwadi, *Carey, Christ and Cultural Transformation* (OM Publishing, 1993), pp. 1-8.

Hindu system, encouraging the poor to learn is encouraging them to sin.'[39]

In a global survey of the impact of Bible translation, it was found that Bible translators 'had a profound effect on the emergence of national consciousness'. By giving peoples a written language of their own, they provided a cultural asset that is then used to keep written records of the various histories and cultures:

> More than 90 percent of these languages have a grammar and dictionary at all only because the Western missionary movement provided them, thus pioneering arguably the largest, most diverse and most vigorous movement of cultural renewal in history. Bible translation has enabled countries to free themselves from colonialism. Often it was the first written form for tribes, giving them the means by which they could put in written form demands and concerns, which for most led to disassociation from their European overlords. Not surprisingly, when one looks at the key moments for decolonization or the recognition of indigenous rights, missionaries and translators are often in the picture.[40]

Baroness Caroline Cox has often visited Burma (Myanmar). She works with local partners, in areas where human rights abuses abound. These partners testify that the Burmese government dislikes Christianity especially because it 'fosters

---

39 Darrow L. Miller and Stan Guthrie, *Discipling Nations: The Power of Truth to Transform Cultures*, p. 68, quoted in Wayne Grudem, *The Poverty of Nations*, p. 255.

40 Brian Stiller, *From Jerusalem to Timbuktu: A World Tour of the Spread of Christianity* (IVP, 2018), p. 63; the quote from Lamin Sanneh, *Disciples of All Nations* (OUP, 2008).

genuine democracy by encouraging individuals to think for themselves.'[41] That is a powerful tribute to the impact of the education promoted by Christians. Similarly, on a trip to a war-torn region of Sudan Caroline Cox was told by one leader that British missionaries had given his people education, which resulted in the freedom to think for themselves.

You cannot give anyone a greater gift or freedom than that.[42]

Further Reading

Vishal Mangalwadi, *The Book that Made Your World, How the Bible Created the Soul of Western Civilisation* (Thomas Nelson, 2011), pp. 77-91; 161-245.

Alvin J. Schmidt, *How Christianity Changed the World* (Zondervan, 2004), pp. 170-93; 218-47.

Rodney Stark, *For the Glory of God: How Monotheism led to Reformations, Science, Witch-hunts and the End of Slavery* (Princeton University Press, 2004), pp. 121-99.

---

41   Caroline Cox, 'Holding the Line', in Lynda Rose, (ed), *What are they Teaching the Children?* (VFJ/Wilberforce Publications, 2016), p. 342.

42   Cox, p. 343.

9 The Creation Mandate and the Value of Work

Lakshmi's husband was an auto rickshaw driver. When he died suddenly, Lakshmi was left without means to provide for herself and her three children. Her parents had earned a living by making baskets. Lakshmi knew how to make baskets, but she had no money to buy stock. As a 'Dalit' in India, her situation seemed hopeless.

Christians in the Dignity Freedom Network[1] secured a business start-up grant for Lakshmi. She was able to buy materials and begin to make and sell baskets. She now earns enough to provide for herself and her three children.[2]

The Creator God made Lakshmi in His own image: she is not just *created*, she is *creative*. The biblical world view offers an inspiring vision of work. It is not just a means by which we survive. When we work, we reflect and honour our Creator.

---

1   As mentioned in chapter one.
2   Dignity Freedom Network, 'Economic Empowerment', https://dfn. org.uk/economic-empowerment (accessed 23 April, 2020). Name changed.

Enabling Lakshmi to run her own small business is more honouring to God, and more fulfilling to her, than simply giving her and her children a daily allowance for food.

Work Demeaned: The Ancient World

Both the Greeks and the Romans saw paid work as fit only for slaves and the lower classes. Greek gods were regarded as those who never had to work. Ancient Greeks thought that manual labour or household tasks were unbefitting a citizen. The ideal for freemen was to have leisure to cultivate the mind. A Greek word corresponding to 'work' was *ascholia*, meaning 'not leisure'. Similarly in Rome, the great philosopher and statesman **Cicero (106-43 BC)** believed that physical labour was vulgar, and working for a living was unbecoming a freeman. He expressed the view of the educated classes:

> That which is most excellent, and is most to be desired by all happy, honest and healthy-minded men, is dignified leisure.[3]

Societies without a world view which insists that all human beings have individual rights (by virtue of being human) have little incentive to exploit technology to make work less backbreaking. The engineers of ancient Egypt were able to construct pyramids in honour of rulers, but did not see the need to make wheelbarrows to make the work any easier for slaves.[4] For centuries Hindus in India believed that a whole

---

3   Cicero, *Pro Publio Sestio*, Chapter XLV, https://en.wikiquote.org/wiki/Cicero (accessed 23 April, 2020).

4   Vishal Mangalwadi, *The Book that Made your World* (Thomas Nelson 2011), p. 93.

caste were on earth in order to serve others. The 'fate' of the Dalits was to carry water, generation after generation.

Mahatma Gandhi opposed technology, but such opposition condemns some people to go on, generation after generation, performing even the most degraded functions. If you can't pump water into homes, then you can't flush toilets. In India the Dalits are often expected to carry away human waste.[5]

Societies which have no inherent belief in human dignity do not acknowledge personal property rights. Those in the elite can appropriate the labour and goods of others for their ends. Those cultures which have a cyclical view of time have little incentive to invest in the future.

Work Dignified: Biblical World View

The biblical view of work begins with the recognition that God Himself works:

> On the seventh day God had finished the work he had been doing; so on the seventh day he rested from all his work. And God blessed the seventh day and made it holy, because on it he rested from all the work of creating that he had done. (Gen. 2:2-3)

When we are told that God formed the man from the dust of the ground (Gen. 2:7), the word 'formed' echoes the potter's skill in shaping clay. When Jesus said, 'My Father is always at his work to this very day, and I, too, am working' (John 5:17),

---

5   Ibid., pp. 94-5.

He was alluding to God's ongoing supervision and control of creation and providence (Ps. 107: 8, 15, 21, 31).

We are made in the image of our Creator God, so too we are created to create.

> And God said: 'Let us make man in our image, after our likeness. And let them have dominion over the fish of the sea and over the birds of heavens and over the livestock and over all the earth and over every creeping thing that creeps on the earth'. (Gen. 1:26, ESV)

God gave humanity a mandate to manage or steward the earth on His behalf (Gen. 1:28). We are called to be responsible and wise in managing and developing the earth's resources. Human ingenuity and hard work are needed in order to fulfil that task well.

Our first parents were called to 'rule over' the rest of the animate creation on behalf of God Himself, the great King. To do that we need to study and understand the creation.

> The earth is the Lord's and everything in it, the world and all who live in it. (Ps. 24:1)

> You made him ruler over the works of your hands; you put all things under his feet: all flocks and herds, and the animals of the wild, the birds in the sky, and the fish in the sea, all that swim the paths of the seas. Oh LORD our Lord, how majestic is your name in all the earth! (Ps. 8:6-9)

The fourth commandment indicates that our work and God's work share the same pattern. The duty to work, and the obligation to rest and honour the Creator, both derive from creation:

> Remember the Sabbath day by keeping it holy. Six days you shall labour and do all your work, but the seventh day is a Sabbath to the LORD your God. On it you shall not do any work, neither you, nor your son or daughter, nor your manservant or maidservant, nor your animals, nor the alien within your gates. For in six days the LORD made the heavens and the earth, the sea, and all that is in them, but he rested on the seventh day. Therefore the LORD blessed the Sabbath day and made it holy. (Exod. 20:8-11)

Since the Fall, we only fulfil the creation mandate imperfectly and incompletely. It will be perfectly fulfilled in Jesus, the ultimate Man (Heb. 2:5-9), and also completely fulfilled in His resurrected followers. But the fall into sin does not nullify the original command. It is inextricably linked with the creation of men and women in the image of God. Humans are still called to:

> ... explore the resources of the earth, to cultivate its land, to mine its buried treasures. Yet we must not think simply about land, plants, and animals; we must also think about human existence itself, insofar as it is an aspect of God's good creation. Man is called by God to develop all the potentialities found in nature and humankind as a whole. He must seek to develop not only agriculture, horticulture and animal husbandry, but also science, technology, and art. In other words, we have here what is often called the

cultural mandate: the command to develop a God-glorifying culture.[6]

Dominion – Not Exploitation

Today, concern for the environment is at the top of the political agenda. Some see biblical Christianity as the enemy of the environment. 'Dominion' is interpreted as 'exploitation'. The Bible is viewed as giving a free pass to environmental degradation and cruelty to animals.

Some radical environmentalists see nothing especially valuable about humanity. They suggest that people gobble up earth's resources, and some suggest that radical measures must be taken to limit human populations, including forced family planning, sterilisation and abortion. Some even advocate genocide.[7]

God created this world as His beautiful domain, and He set our first parents as His 'deputies' or 'regents' to manage it for Him. Responsible stewards manage their master's possessions carefully. They do not unnecessarily spoil or waste or destroy the resources they have been entrusted with. When Adam and Eve were told to 'steward' the earth's resources, that implied they were to manage them well. They would answer to their Creator for any wilful damage or needless waste. But God placed resources in the earth to be used for human benefit.

6   Anthony A. Hoekema, *Created in God's Image* (Grand Rapids: Eerdmans, 1986), p. 79.

7   Pentti Linkola, *Human Flood*, 1989, translated by H. Heinonen and M. Moynihan http://www.penttilinkola.com/pentti_linkola/ ecofascism_writings/humanflood/ (accessed 26 March 2020).

Minerals were not to just lie in the ground. The land was not just to lie uncultivated. Seeds were to be sown and grown, and to bear a harvest. The garden was to be cultivated. As human beings 'filled' the earth, they would eventually be able to bring the whole earth to its potential. All the rich resources of earth and sea were for human enjoyment, but this would also result in blessing for all creation.

The personal God placed people *over* the rest of creation. Humans are created, we are 'creatures', but we are not just 'creatures' like animals. We are personal because we are made in God's image. It is right to 'privilege' humanity above the rest of creation. Jesus taught that we are of 'more value' than birds (Matt. 6:26) or animals (Matt. 12:12). It is right to use the rest of creation for the benefit of people. God does not just intend humans to survive, but to flourish (Deut. 28:1-14). But there should be no needless cruelty (Prov. 12:10) or needless damage to the inanimate creation (Num. 35:33-4; Deut. 20:19). God owns the earth (1 Chron. 29:11), and He cares how human beings look after it. Moreover, God has undertaken to care for His creation (Gen. 9:1-11). That perspective is overlooked or denied by those radical environmentalists who fear that the world will run out of resources.[8]

After the Fall, the fulfilment of the creation mandate would be attended with toil, both in working the ground and in filling the earth (Gen. 3:16-19). But humans were still to honour their Creator by doing both. After the Fall, animals were killed in order to make clothing (Gen. 3: 21), and after

---

8   See also Wayne Grudem and Barry Asmus, *The Poverty of Nations* (Crossway, 2013), p. 339.

the Flood Noah and his family were told that they could use animals for food (Gen. 9:3).[9]

Some have a romantic notion of the 'unspoiled' life people live in subsistence economies. But when this was the global norm life-expectancy was less than thirty years. In two hundred years life-expectancy globally more than doubled due to the agricultural and industrial revolutions.[10] During the 1980s I spent two years volunteering in one of the poorest nations on earth, and saw how cruel it is to idealise life in a society where infant mortality is around fifty per cent, and life-expectancy is less than fifty years.

A biblical world view steers a course between the two wrong extremes. One is the idea that elevates the ecosystem over humans, which can lead to the demand to eliminate humans to 'save' the earth. This ignores the special dignity of humankind as created in God's image. The other extreme is to say that we can control the natural world for our own benefit. That world view also ignores God, who created the earth and delights in it (Gen. 1; Job 38-42).

In summary we are to develop the earth for human blessing, but all is to be for the glory of God. The natural world must be managed wisely with a view to future generations.

Working for the King

As human beings we are answerable to the great King for *how* we fulfil this creation calling. God is pleased with good work,

---

9   There were certain qualifications, and food laws were given to the nation of Israel. In the New Testament, these were abrogated.

10   Grudem and Asmus, p. 110.

and displeased with shoddy, lazy or poorly executed work. The book of Proverbs teaches that the fear of God leads to wisdom in everyday relationships and tasks. Character traits such as honesty, reliability, cheerfulness, insight, all have direct relevance to effective work. All people will have to answer to God for how we work, but Christians have the added incentive of knowing that we work to honour our Saviour:

> Whatever you do, work at it with all your heart, as working for the Lord, not for men, since you know that you will receive an inheritance from the Lord as a reward. It is the Lord Christ you are serving. (Col. 3:23-4)

The early Christians remembered that Jesus Christ grew up in a carpenter's home, and worked until He began His public ministry, around the age of thirty (Mark 6:3). They recalled that the apostle Paul was willing to support himself by means of tent-making (Acts 18:3). A Christian handbook written around 375, *The Apostolic Constitutions*, stated:

> ... mind your business with all becoming seriousness, that so you may always have sufficient to support yourselves and those that are needy, and not burden the Church of God. For we ourselves, besides our attention to the word of the Gospel, do not neglect our inferior employments. For some of us are fishermen, some tent makers, some husband-men, that so we may never be idle. So says Solomon somewhere: 'Go to the ant, thou sluggard' (Prov. 6:6; 12:11; 19:24; Eccles. 4:5; 10:18). But 'if any one does not work, let not such a one eat'

(2 Thess. 3:10). For the Lord our God hates the slothful. For no-one of those who are dedicated to God ought to be idle.[11]

The early Christians took from Scripture a work ethic that gave dignity to everyday occupations. In addition, the biblical world view is that time is linear, not cyclical. There is progress through time and we can develop the earth's resources to bring blessing to others and to future generations. While God is the ultimate Creator and owner of all, He ordains that people's possessions should be respected. The eighth commandment is: 'You shall not steal'. Even a poor person should not have their cloak or essential work tools taken as guarantee for a loan (Exod. 22:26-7; Deut. 24: 6,10,13). Boundary markers were to be respected (Deut. 19:14). History shows that respect for personal property rights is essential to provide incentive for productive work.[12]

The Monasteries and Technological Innovation

Rome prospered by means of extracting tribute from subject nations. When the Roman Empire collapsed, millions of people were liberated from having to pay high taxes to a centralised authority, which led to greater freedom for

---

11   *The Apostolic Constitutions*, Section VIII, 'On the Duty of Working for a Livelihood. That a Christian Who Will Not Work Must Not Eat, as Peter and the Rest of the Apostles Were Fishermen, But Paul and Aquila Tentmakers, Jude the Son of James an Husbandman', https://ccel.org/ccel/schaff/anf07/anf07.ix.iii.viii.html (accessed 24 April, 2020).

12   Alvin J. Schmidt, *How Christianity Changed the World* (Zondervan, 2004), pp. 202-4; 211-12; Grudem and Asmus pp. 114-16; 141-54.

entrepreneurial innovation.[13] From the sixth century onwards, the Benedictine monks saw productive labour as a part of their service. During subsequent centuries, other monastic orders arose. The monasteries were the source of major technological innovations. Labour-saving machines were developed in Christian monasteries because of the biblical assumption of the worth of every human, and a reluctance to needlessly subject people to monotonous toil.[14] This world view lay behind the astonishing range of technical advance in Europe:

> In architecture, engineering, machinery, agronomy, and the exploitation of new sources of power, the Middle Ages were marked by periods of invention far more prolonged, creative and diverse than any known to Hellenistic, Roman or Islamic culture. We may find it somewhat difficult now to appreciate the revolutionary implications of devices like the heavy saddle with stirrups, the wheeled plough, the rigid horse collar, heavy armour, and the nailed horseshoe, but they allowed for the cultivation of soils that had never before been genuinely arable, helped initiate a long period of Western military security and did much to foster the kind of economic and demographic growth for want of which the Western Roman Empire had fallen into ruin ... Waterwheels appeared ... first as simple watermills, but then with the ever more sophisticated use of gears, as engines of mechanised industry, most particularly in the Cistercian monasteries of the twelfth century and after. In these monasteries, waterpower was used not only to grind and sift grain, but to drive hammers on cam shafts for the

---

13   Rodney Stark, *The Victory of Reason* (Random House, 2006), p. 36.
14   Mangalwadi, p. 95.

fulling of wool, to prepare leather for tanning, to run oil presses and wood saws and the bellows of furnaces, and so on. The abundant production of wrought iron and finally of cast iron ... constant improvements in the technology of mining ... the invention and refinement of the windmill; the development of sophisticated earthenware and glass glazing; the flying buttress and the Gothic arch; discoveries in the geometry of refraction and the consequent perfection of magnifying lenses for eyeglasses; the birth and continuous refinement of the mechanical clock; the development of large seafaring vessels with rudders supported on sternposts and sails so rigged as to allow complete exploitation of the winds; the invention of the magnetic compass – all of these among many more, were special achievements of Western medieval culture. And no previous culture had ever boasted technological advances of such scope and variety.[15]

In 1905, German sociologist Max Weber published *The Protestant Ethic and the Spirit of Capitalism*. This popularised the concept of the 'Protestant work ethic'. It is more helpful to think in terms of a 'Christian work ethic' or a 'biblical work ethic'. The Bible teaches that we are created to create, that there is dignity in work, and that we are to work (and rest) for God's glory. Wealth creation did not begin with Protestantism. It began with the creation mandate. Although creation is tainted by sin, Christians still demonstrate that we can love God, serve our fellow human beings and responsibly manage the rest of creation as we work for God's glory on His earth.

---

15 David Bentley Hart, *Atheist Delusions: The Christian Revolution and its Fashionable Enemies* (Yale University Press, 2010), pp. 72-3.

Business for the Glory of God

The Reformation did, however, lead to a deeper appreciation of the biblical concept of 'vocation'. Martin Luther, for example, insisted that the humblest occupation can be done for the glory of God and the good of others, and that there is an inherent dignity in that. Work is the 'mask of God': He is in it, although hidden. Of course since the fall into sin work is often frustrating and difficult (Gen. 3:17-19). But it is still significant.

Christianity has a great history of entrepreneurs, who have used their gifts, abilities, energy and resources for the good of others, and ultimately for the glory of God.

God is the giver of those capacities. While, ultimately, the whole earth belongs to God and we are only His stewards, we *are* His stewards, and He expects us to develop it for the common good.

Josiah Wedgwood (1730-1795) revolutionised the early modern factory system. He treated workers with dignity, and expected high standards in return. The factory produced at an extraordinary level of both quality and quantity. He provided excellent products, jobs for many workers, and financed the anti-slavery movement. His company made and subsidised the price of countless anti-slavery medallions which were a wildly popular way of publicising the cause.

The Quaker movement started as a revival movement in the seventeenth century.[16] In subsequent years, they, along with others who couldn't in conscience conform to the

---

16   Many Quakers now are theologically very liberal.

established Church, were not allowed to go to university. They were also not allowed to serve in any public office. Many threw themselves into business instead. Household names include Cadbury of Birmingham, Fry's of Bristol, Rowntree's and Terry's of York; Barclays and Lloyds banks, Clarks shoes, Bryant & May matches and the biscuit firms Huntley & Palmers and Carrs. By 1851, Quakers only represented 0.1 per cent of the population of Britain, but they were enormously significant in business. They put biblical principles into practice, treating workers with dignity, giving buyers an excellent product and a fair price, keeping their word and paying bills on time.

Quakers dominated the chocolate business because they aimed to produce an alternative to the misery and deprivation caused by alcohol. Cocoa was a way of providing an alternative cheap, appealing and widely available drink. It was healthy because you had to boil the water to make it in a situation where often water supplies were contaminated.

Famously, the village of Bournville was built outside Birmingham for Cadbury's workers: it provided schools, leisure facilities and parks, doctors and dentists. Each house had a garden. Cadbury was one of the first firms to make pension provisions and provide a workers' canteen.

Cyrus McCormick (1809-1884) was an American inventor and businessman whose vision was to invent a machine which would help eliminate world hunger. He founded a Harvesting Machine Company which enabled vastly increased productivity. By 1850 it could truly be said that 'McCormick brings bread to the mouths of the poor.'[17] This was done by liberating labourers from mindless toil and by enhancing human productivity through machines. In 1878 the French government awarded McCormick a national honour, saying that he'd done more for agriculture than anyone else alive.

McCormick was a radically innovative entrepreneur who ended up making $10 million. Profits were saved and reinvested in the company, or else given to Christian and philanthropic work. In 1869, for example, he gave $10,000 to help the American evangelist Dwight Moody start the Young Men's Christian Association. A devout Presbyterian McCormick exemplified self-denial, sobriety, thriftiness, efficiency, and morality. He made a fortune, but much of it was given to Kingdom purposes. He helped feed people on earth, but also laid up treasure in heaven. After his death, his widow Nettie continued his Christian and charitable activities. She donated $8 million (over $160 million in modern equivalents) to hospitals, disaster and relief agencies, churches, youth activities and educational institutions.

Another godly entrepreneur was **John Laing (1879-1978)**. Born in Carlisle, England, John's father, grandfather and great grandfather had all been in the construction business. The family were devout Brethren. John professed conversion when he was seven years old, and left school aged fourteen. Although his father owned the business, he started at the bottom, as an apprentice, where he had to work long hours, in harsh conditions, alongside all the other construction

---

17   Mangalwadi, p. 213.

workers. Later, when managing the company, he understood working conditions. He never went to university, but taught himself in his spare time. Aged just nineteen he was given the huge responsibility of supervising the building of the first power station in the north-west of England.[18]

Aged twenty-nine, John took over the management of the family business. During the second world war, although by then he was sixty-five years of age, he devoted himself and the company's resources to the war effort. After the war Laing's major projects included the building of the first motorway in Britain, and the repair of war-damaged Coventry Cathedral.

Laing always put God first, and he retained the basic standard of living he'd started out with. By 1940 he was giving away £20,000 a year (today's equivalent would be £1 million). He ploughed immense sums into student Christian work. He bought the UCCF London headquarters, as well as the Christian Union base in Oxford. When he died in 1978 although he had presided over a multi-million pound company, his personal estate was valued at just £371.

Laing dismissed lazy or incompetent workers, but was generous if there was genuine hardship. He introduced new practices such as holiday pay and a pension scheme at a time when working conditions in the building industry were often terrible. Alongside running the business he was an elder in his Brethren Assembly, ran a men's Bible study group, and enjoyed doing occasional open air preaching. He went on Crusader camps until he was seventy.

---

18   Garry J. Williams, *Silent Witnesses* (Banner of Truth, 2013), p. 143.

Reflecting God's Self-Giving Love in Our Daily Work

Whether as a leading entrepreneur, or as the humblest of office workers, joy and meaning can be found in work when there is the attitude that work is not ultimately about 'me' but about serving God and others.

Greg Foster tells of a relative, raised in the Church, who walked away from the faith at an early age. Fifty years later she became a Christian. For many years she had worked in an office, holding down a burdensome, repetitive job. Christians were the only people who came into work happy to be there. They were focused on how they were blessing people in their work instead of thinking about themselves. Their attitude pointed others toward the supernatural power that had changed them. She wanted that for herself, testifying: *I believe Jesus is alive, because I've seen how he works in people's lives.*[19] She was so impressed with the attitude of her Christian colleagues, because it contrasted so powerfully with our current culture which assumes that our ultimate goal is self-fulfilment.

In 1979, American sociologist Christopher Lasch wrote a best-selling book entitled *The Culture of Narcissism*. He demonstrated that until the mid-twentieth century a work ethic based on Christian values had underpinned Western culture. There was a respect for industry, sobriety, moderation, self-discipline, and avoidance of debt. There was an assumption that it was virtuous to defer gratification, to avoid

---

19   Greg Forster and Tim Keller, *Joy for the World: How Christianity lost its Cultural Influence and can begin rebuilding it* (Crossway, 2014), pp. 109-10.

unnecessary self-indulgence, and to provide for the future of one's family. Gratification was found in caring for others. Lasch charted the lurch towards an emphasis on individual and instant gratification, and a diminishing emphasis on self-denial and hard work.[20] He described the 'Puritan sense of calling' as teaching that every Christian had a general calling to serve God and a personal calling, by which he or she could discern what particular area of work to pursue. God has created humans to be sociable and to serve others. This perspective equipped people to cope with either adversity or prosperity with relative equanimity. Personal aggrandisement was viewed as secondary to the social good. There was a common understanding that each person was part of a wider societal endeavour: 'the collective transformation of nature and the progress of useful arts and useful knowledge'.[21] That culture has collapsed into a culture where increasingly it's 'all about me'. The biblical work ethic offers something far more satisfying.

A Biblical View of Work Leads to Human Flourishing

Today it's common to find a suspicion of wealth creation among many evangelicals. Of course work can become an idol, and wealth can be a snare. But the fact that something good can be abused does not negate its worth. If we truly love our neighbour we should be distressed by the terrible poverty

20　Christopher Lasch, *The Culture of Narcissism: American Life in an Age of Diminishing Expectations* (Norton & Co, 1979), p. 53.

21　Ibid., p. 54.

suffered by great numbers of people in so many nations. The only way to lift nations out of poverty is for them to increase their production of goods and services and for enterprise to be encouraged and facilitated. Human skill, energy and diligence are qualities given to human beings to enable them to fulfil the creation mandate. They are God-given and to be encouraged.[22]

Global poverty has dramatically decreased over the past two hundred years, at the same time as enormous population growth. The proportion of people living in extreme income poverty worldwide plunged from forty-three per cent in 1990 to twenty-two per cent in 2008.[23] Economist Deirdre McCloskey comments:

> Never had such a thing happened. Count it in your head: eight and a half times more actual food and clothing and housing and education and travel and books for the average human being—even though there were six times more of them.[24]

When you analyse how this has happened, it has been by means of encouraging human enterprise. Humans are not a problem to be eliminated (*contra* the extreme environmentalists). Our

---

22 Grudem and Asmus, also Wayne Grudem, *Business for the Glory of God: The Bible's Teaching on the Moral Goodness of Business* (Crossway, 2003).

23 James R. Rogers, 'What's Behind the Stunning Decrease in Global Poverty?' *First Things*, 26 November, 2013, https://www.firstthings.com/web-exclusives/2013/11/whats-behind-the-stunning-decrease-in-global-poverty (accessed 24 April, 2020).

24 Deirdre McCloskey, *The Bourgeois Virtues: Ethics for an Age of Commerce* (University of Chicago Press, 2007), p. 16.

God-given capacities offer the best solution to world poverty and other challenges to human well-being.

Wayne Grudem and Barry Asmus argue that when biblical principles are followed, a culture conducive to wealth creation is fostered:

> The cultural values of a nation determine what kind of economic system it adopts, what kinds of laws and policies the government enacts, whether corruption is tolerated, whether freedoms are protected, and what kinds of goals individuals set for their personal lives.[25]

By contrast, the twentieth century saw a great and disastrous experiment in running countries according to atheistic Marxism. Denying that human beings are made in the image of God led to the dehumanising of millions of people. R. J. Rummel described the grim results:

> And what did Marxism, this greatest of human social experiments, achieve for its poor citizens, at this most bloody cost in lives? Nothing positive. It left in its wake an economic, environmental, social and cultural disaster ... The irony is that in practice, even after decades of total control, Marxism did not improve the lot of the average person, but usually made living conditions worse than before the revolution. It is not by chance that the world's greatest famines have happened within the Soviet Union (about 5 million dead from 1921-23 and 7 million from 1932-3, including 2 million outside Ukraine) and communist China (about 30 million dead from 1959-61). Overall, in the last century almost 55 million people died in various Marxist

---

25   Grudem and Asmus, p. 309.

famines and associated epidemics – a little over 10 million of them were intentionally starved to death, and the rest died as an unintended result of Marxist collectivization and agricultural policies.

What is astonishing is that this 'currency' of death by Marxism is not thousands or even hundreds of thousands, but millions of deaths. This is almost incomprehensible – it is as though the whole population of the American New England and Middle Atlantic States, or California and Texas, had been wiped out. And that around 35 million people escaped Marxist countries as refugees was an unequalled vote against Marxist utopian pretensions. Its equivalent would be everyone fleeing California, emptying it of all human beings.[26]

Created to Create: 'Let Us Give Wings to Truth'

Atheistic Marxism led to a wasteland of human deprivation and misery. It failed wretchedly.

Still, today many deny the existence of our Creator. But we should be joyful and confident as we remember that we are not here by chance. We are made in the image of God, and we are created to create.

The goldsmith, printer and publisher **Johannes Gutenberg (1400-1468)** was born in the German city of Mainz. In 1450 he invented the printing press. The first book off his press was

---

26   R. J. Rummel, 'The Killing Machine that is Marxism', *The Schwarz Report*, 15 December, 2004, https://www.schwarzreport.org/resources/essays/the-killing-machine-that-is-marxism (accessed 8 April, 2020).

the Bible.[27] For centuries scribes had exhausted themselves in laboriously copying manuscripts. A copy of the Bible had taken a year to produce by hand. Gutenberg delighted in the fact that there was now a machine which 'never wearies'. He wanted to 'give wings to truth'. Within ten years the total number of books in the world went from fifty thousand to over ten million.

The diligence, curiosity, inventiveness and industry of Johannes Gutenberg were all qualities which reflected some of the attributes of God Himself. Affirming and encouraging creativity, diligence, innovation and enterprise leads to human flourishing. Above all, it glorifies God.

Further Reading

Wayne Grudem, *Business to the Glory of God* (Crossway, 2003).

Wayne Grudem and Barry Asmus, *The Poverty of Nations* (Crossway 2013), pp. 114-16; 141-54; 250-52; 280-84; 335-7.

John L. Mackay, *The Dignity of Work*, www.christian.org.uk/wp-content/uploads/dignityofwork.pdf

Vishal Mangalwadi, *The Book that Made your World* (Thomas Nelson, 2011), pp. 92-115; 315-33.

Alvin J. Schmidt, *How Christianity Changed the World* (Zondervan, 2004), pp. 194-215.

---

27   Printing had been known in China, but presses had never been widely manufactured before.

Rodney Stark, *The Victory of Reason: How Christianity led to Freedom, Capitalism and Western Success* (Random House, 2006), pp. 35-63.

10 History: The Triumph of Christ

'New atheists' look back at history and argue that Christianity has been an oppressive and toxic influence: imperialist, cruel, persecuting and 'patriarchal'. The late Christopher Hitchens (1949-2011) wrote a book with the title: *God is not Great*, and the subtitle *How Religion poisons everything* (2007). And Richard Dawkins famously said that:

> Faith is one of the world's great evils, comparable to the smallpox virus but harder to eradicate.[1]

In reality, as Dr William Provine explained in 1994, when you eradicate faith, you rule out meaning and purpose in history:

> Let me summarize my views on what modern evolutionary biology tells us loud and clear – and these are basically Darwin's views. There are no gods, no purposes, and no goal-directed forces of any kind. There is no life after death. When I die, I am absolutely certain that I am going to be

---

1   Richard Dawkins, *The Humanist*, 57, January/February 1997. He was speaking of 'faith' in general, including Christianity.

dead. That's the end of me. There is no ultimate foundation for ethics, no ultimate meaning in life, and no free will for humans, either.[2]

A materialist world view leaves no space for final judgement and the righting of wrongs. Evil won't be called to account. There is no foundation for determining what is evil or good. This removes any foundation for justice or compassion. The atheist and materialist world view doesn't allow for any overarching purpose in history. The biblical view is very different.

The History of Redemption

One Sunday in March 1739 a ten-year-old boy called Nehemiah Strong took his seat in the new church building in Northampton, Massachusetts. His pastor, the great American revival preacher Jonathan Edwards, read out two verses from Isaiah 51:

> Fear not the reproach of man,
> nor be dismayed at their reviling.
> For the moth will eat them up like a garment,
> and the worm will eat them like wool;
> > *but my righteousness will be for ever,*
> > *and my salvation to all generations.* (Isa. 51:7-8)

Between March and August, Jonathan Edwards preached thirty sermons on those verses under the title *The History of Redemption*.[3] The little boy, Nehemiah would go on to become a professor of

---

2   William Provine in debate with Phillip Johnson, Stanford University, April 30, 1994, http://www.arn.org/docs/orpages/or161/161main. htm (accessed 1 May, 2020).

3   Jonathan Edwards, *The History of Redemption*, 1739 (rep. The Sovereign Grace Book Club, 1959).

mathematics and natural philosophy at Yale. In later years he looked back on that sermon series as one of the great events of his life.[4] He recalled his increasing excitement as Jonathan Edwards put before his congregation a stunning overview of history from Creation to the Second Coming. Where is history going? What is it all about? Is it just a random series of events? Edwards showed from Scripture that the history of the world is the history of Redemption. History is not a meaningless cycle of rise and fall, misery and relief. There is a cosmic conflict going on between God's Kingdom, and the forces of darkness, but victory was won at Calvary. The little stone which smashes ungodly empires is filling, and will fill, the whole earth.[5]

In the Puritan tradition, Edwards had confidence that Christ is reigning until all enemies are placed under His feet (1 Cor. 15:25).[6] In 1738 he had preached a sermon on that text entitled 'Christ gloriously exalted over all evil'.[7] In it he argued that all the hideous manifestations of evil in history were, are, and will be only the occasion for Christ's glory to triumph. Yes, new manifestations of evil will arise until Christ comes again. The Bible is realistic about ongoing suffering and persecution, as well as giving us great promises of blessing to claim in prayer. But we are not to give way to sinful discouragement.

---

4   George M. Marsden, *Jonathan Edwards, A Life* (Yale University Press, 2003), p. 195.

5   Marsden, p. 488; Stephen J. Nichols, *A Time For Confidence* (Reformation Trust, 2016), pp. 112-16.

6   Iain Murray, *The Puritan Hope* (Banner of Truth, 1971).

7   Jonathan Edwards, 'Christ Exalted', 1738, https://www.biblebb. com/files/edwards/exalted.htm (accessed 1 May, 2020).

One summer's evening in August 1875, the great London preacher Charles Haddon Spurgeon also chose to preach on 1 Corinthians 15:25.[8] He reflected that when Christ told His disciples that 'The Son of Man must suffer' (Mark 8:31), they didn't believe Him. They could only conceive that the Son of Man should reign, not suffer! Spurgeon went on to argue that the sin of unbelief had been reversed. Believers in his day were so accustomed to seeing Christ's cause derided, they could only conceive that His cause in this age must be weak. But the testimony of Scripture is that Christ is indeed King (Ps. 110:2).

As in Spurgeon's day, many evangelicals today in the Western world are paralysed with discouragement. There are mountains of evil and often it seems that Satan is conquering. Many gloomily predict that the prospects for Christ's Kingdom in this age can only get worse. The first section of the Lord's Prayer: 'Hallowed be Your Name, Your Kingdom Come, Your will be done on earth as it is in Heaven', if prayed at all, is prayed with little hope of any fulfilment in this age. The prospect of Scripture promises ever being fulfilled are pushed into the age to come.

But Christ is King. He triumphed over every evil at the cross. The horror of each evil only serves to magnify the splendour of His triumph. And Christ triumphs over Satan's wretched and miserable kingdom in the present age through His body, His people. We are called to share the gospel, and we are called to stand for God's righteousness and protect the

---

8   Charles H. Spurgeon, 'He Must Reign', Sermon on 1 Corinthians 15:25, Lord's Day Evening, 18 August, 1875, Sermon no. 2940 preached at the Metropolitan Tabernacle.

weak and defenceless. We can thank God for all those, some of them mentioned in this book, who have obeyed this call.

And Christ triumphs gloriously through the prayers of His people. Jonathan Edwards saw this clearly. He published *An Humble Attempt* in 1746, a challenge to God's people to unite in prayer for the evangelisation of the world.[9] His vision was picked up by William Carey, who published the *Enquiry into the Obligation of Christians to use Means for the Conversion of the Heathen* in 1792.[10] This was a carefully researched handbook of the extent of gospel progress in every nation of the world to date, and a summons to pray for and evangelise the unreached nations. Many churches and individuals responded to the appeal. Their prayers were wonderfully answered in the worldwide expansion of Christianity over the next two centuries.

Later in the nineteenth century, many Christians committed to pray for China which seemed unreachable. Their prayers bore untold fruit in the twentieth century. In the mid-twentieth century, united prayer went up on behalf of persecuted Christians behind the 'Iron Curtain'. It seemed that oppression would never end. But in 1989 communism in Eastern European countries collapsed, seemingly as easily as an old garment falls to bits when devoured by moths:

> The moth will eat them up like a garment, *but my salvation lasts from generation to generation.* (Isa. 51:8)

---

9   Jonathan Edwards, *A Call to United Extraordinary Prayer* ('An Humble Attempt'), (Christian Focus, 2004).

10   William Carey, *An Enquiry into the Obligations of Christians to use Means for the Conversion of the Heathen,* Leicester, 1792, https://www.wmcarey.edu/carey/enquiry/anenquiry.pdf (accessed 1 May, 2020).

We dishonour God when we allow the challenges of our day to push us into a defensive, timid and pessimistic mindset, afraid to speak and stand for truth. All those who have been most dynamic in Church history, have been confident in the promises of God.

> The earth *will* be filled with the knowledge of the glory of God as the waters cover the sea (Hab. 2:14; Isa. 11:9).

> God's name *will* be great among the nations from the rising to the setting of the sun (Mal. 1:11).

We can be confident in God and in His good purposes for history! We long for the return of our Lord Jesus. We know that at that Day every knee will finally bow to Him. But until He returns we are not content to see whole nations in bondage to false systems of thought which keep people away from Christ. We want to see God glorified in every place, and we want to reach out to proclaim the good news of the gospel and to show Christ's love as we love our neighbour.

As we look back, we admit that human sin has often spoiled the testimony of God's people. There is no room for pride. But by God's grace, His people have often had a transformative effect. We've touched on just a few episodes of that story. And as we look forward, along with those believers who have gone before, some of whom we've remembered in this book, we can be certain that the future is 'as bright as the promises of God'.[11]

---

11   Quoting Adoniram Judson. F. Wayland, *Pulling the Eye Tooth from a Live Tiger, A Memoir of Adoniram Judson*, volume 2, 1853 (rep. Audubon Press, 2006), p. 381.

Further Resources

Thomas Andrew, *The Church and the Charter* (Theos, 2014), pp. 37-9, https://www.theosthinktank.co.uk/cmsfiles/archive/files/Reports/The%20Church%20and%20the%20Charter.pdf (accessed 28 April, 2020).

David Bentley Hart, *Atheist Delusions: The Christian Revolution and Its Fashionable Enemies* (Yale University Press, 2010).

Stephen Brown, 'Sydenham: The Physician', *Nucleus*, Spring 1996, Christian Medical Fellowship, https://www.cmf.org.uk/resources/publications/content/?context=article&id=529 (accessed 16 April, 2020).

Daniel Darling, *The Dignity Revolution: Reclaiming God's Rich Vision for Humanity* (The Good Book Company, 2018).

Brian Edwards, *Revival: A People Saturated with God* (Evangelical Press, Day One, 2019).

Jonathan Edwards, *History of Redemption* (Banner of Truth, 2003).

Jonathan Edwards, *Christ Exalted*, *www.biblebb.com/files/edwards/exalted.htm*

Hugh Flemming, 'Post-Hippocratic Medicine: The Problem and the Solution: How the Christian Ethic has influenced Health Care', Kuyper Foundation, 2010, https://www.kuyper.org/s/TextPost-HippocraticMedicine.pdf (accessed 17 April, 2020).

Steve Fouch, 'Care and Compassion', *CMF Files* No. 50, Spring 2013, https://www.cmf.org.uk/resources/publications/content/?context=article&id=26045 (accessed 17 April, 2020).

Luke Goodrich, *Free To Believe: The Battle over Religious Liberty in America* (Multnomah, 2019).

Wayne Grudem and Barry Asmus, *The Poverty of Nations: A Sustainable Solution* (Crossway, 2013).

Wayne Grudem, *Business for the Glory of God* (Crossway, 2003).

Os Guinness, *Renaissance: The Power of the Gospel However Dark the Times* (IVP, 2014).

Kyle Harper, *From Shame to Sin: The Christian Transformation of Sexual Morality in Late Antiquity* (Harvard University Press, 2013).

Gary A. Haugen, *Good News about Injustice* (IVP, 2009).

Gary A. Haugen, *The Locust Effect: Why the End of Poverty Requires the End of Violence* (Oxford University Press, 2014).

Kathleen Heasman, *Evangelicals in Action: An Appraisal of their Social Work* (Geoffry Bles, 1962).

Allen D. Hertzke and Thomas S. Shah, (eds.) *Christianity and Freedom*: Volume I Historical Perspectives; Volume II Contemporary Perspectives (Cambridge University Press, 2016).

Gertrude Himmelfarb, *One Nation, Two Cultures: A Searching Examination of American Society in the Aftermath of Our Cultural Revolution* (Vintage, 2001).

Tom Holland, *Dominion: The Making of the Western Mind* (Little, Brown, 2019).

William Huang, 'Give credit where credit's due: the Christian background to China's best hospitals', *Mercator Net*, 24 March, 2020, https://mercatornet.com/give-credit-where-credits-due-the-christian-background-to-chinas-best-hospitals/47079/ (accessed 15 April 2020).

Sharon James, *God's Design for Women in an Age of Gender Confusion* (Evangelical Press, 2019).

Sharon James, *Gender Ideology: What do Christians need to know?* (Christian Focus, 2019).

Sharon James, *Ann Judson* (Evangelical Press, 2016).

Jeremiah J. Johnston, *Unimaginable: What our World would be like without Christianity* (Bethany House, 2017).

John R. Ling, *When does Human Life Begin?* The Christian Institute, https://www.christian.org.uk/wp-content/uploads/when-does-human-life-begin.pdf (accessed 17 November, 2020).

John R. Ling, *Bioethical Issues*, Day One, 2014.

John L. Mackay, *The Dignity of Work*, The Christian Institute, https://www.christian.org.uk/wp-content/uploads/dignityofwork.pdf (accessed 17 November, 2020).

Vishal Mangalwadi, *The Book that Made your World: How the Bible Created the Soul of Western Civilisation* (Thomas Nelson, 2011).

Vishal and Ruth Mangalwadi, *The Legacy of William Carey: A Model for the Transformation of Culture* (O.M.,1999).

Vishal Mangalwadi, *This Book Changed Everything: The Bible's Amazing Impact on Our World* (Museum of the Bible Books, 2019).

Douglas Murray, *The Strange Death of Europe: Immigration, Identity, Islam* (Bloomsbury Continuum, 2017).

Douglas Murray, *The Madness of Crowds: Gender, Race and Identity* (Bloomsbury Continuum, 2019).

Iain Murray, *The Puritan Hope* (Banner of Truth, 1971).

M. Pickhaver, 'Walking in Good Works: The Sarah Martin Story', *Evangelical Times*, August 2015, https://www.evangelical-times. org/19810/walking-in-good-works-the-sarah-martin-story/ (accessed 17 November, 2020).

Frank K. Prochaska, *Women and Philanthropy in 19th Century England* (Oxford University Press, 1980).

Frank K. Prochaska, *Christianity and Social Service in Modern Britain* (Oxford University Press, 2006).

Lynda Rose,(ed.), *What are They Teaching the Children?* (VFJ/ Wilberforce Publications, 2016).

Matthew Rueger, *Sexual Morality in a Christless World* (Concordia Publishing, 2016).

R. J. Rummel, 'The Killing Machine that is Marxism', *The Schwarz Report*, 15 December, 2004, https://www.schwarzreport.org/ resources/essays/the-killing-machine-that-is-marxism (accessed 8 April, 2020).

Peter Saunders, 'Medicine and the Reformation', *Triple Helix*, Autumn 2017, Christian Medical Fellowship, https://www. cmf.org.uk/resources/publications/content/?context=article &id=26701 (accessed 16 April, 2020).

Francis A. Schaeffer and C. Everett Koop, *Whatever happened to the Human Race?* (Marshall, Morgan and Scott, 1980).

Francis A. Schaeffer, *How Should we then Live? The Rise and Decline of Western Thought and Culture* (Crossway, 1976).

Alvin J. Schmidt, *How Christianity Changed the World* (Zondervan, 2004).

Larry Siedentop, *Inventing the Individual: The Origins of Western Liberalism* (Penguin, 2015).

Ian Shaw, *The Greatest is Charity: The Life of Andrew Reed, preacher and philanthropist* (Evangelical Press, 2005).

Nick Spencer, *Atheists: The Origin of the Species* (Bloomsbury, 2014).

Rodney Stark, *The Rise of Christianity* (HarperCollins, 1997).

Rodney Stark, *For the Glory of God: How Monotheism Led to Reformations, Science, Witch-Hunts, and the End of Slavery* (Princeton University Press, 2004).

Rodney Stark, *The Victory of Reason: How Christianity led to Freedom, Capitalism and Western Success* (Random House, 2006).

Rodney Stark, *The Triumph of Christianity* (Bravo, 2012).

Rodney Stark, *Bearing False Witness: Debunking Centuries of Anti-Catholic History* (Templeton Press, 2016).

Brian Stiller, *From Jerusalem to Timbuktu: A World Tour of the Spread of Christianity* (IVP, 2018).

Ruth Tucker, *From Jerusalem to Irian Jaya: A Biographical History of Christian Missions* (Zondervan, 2004).

Richard Turnbull, *Shaftesbury: The Great Reformer* (Lion, 2010).

Robert L. Wilken, *Liberty in the Things of God* (Yale University Press, 2019).

Garry J. Williams, *Silent Witnesses: Lessons on Theology, Life and the Church from Christians of the Past* (Banner of Truth, 2013), (Life of John Laing).

John Wyatt, *Matters of Life and Death: Human Dilemmas in the light of the Christian Faith* (IVP, 2009).

Also available from Christian Focus Publications...

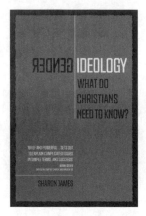

Gender Ideology

What Do Christians Need to Know?

SHARON JAMES

The world has embraced the idea that gender is something that can be decided by individuals. As Christians encounter colleagues, friends and family members who identify as a gender other than the one they were born, we need to be informed and equipped with knowledge about what the issues are, what different terms mean and what the Bible has to say about these things. While we walk the line between loving our neighbour and not buying into the world's lies, Sharon James helps us in this informative and practical guide.

This is a remarkable book, both for the range of material covered and its sharp insights into the dominant pathologies of our time. ... a book from which all parents, pastors, and the Christian public in general will greatly benefit.

Carl R. Trueman
Professor of Biblical and Religious Studies, Grove City College,
Pennsylvania

ISBN 978-1-5271-0481-5

TRUTHFORLIFE®
THE BIBLE-TEACHING MINISTRY OF **ALISTAIR BEGG**

The mission of Truth For Life is to teach the Bible with clarity and relevance so that unbelievers will be converted, believers will be established, and local churches will be strengthened.

Daily Program
Each day, Truth For Life distributes the Bible teaching of Alistair Begg across the U.S. and in several locations outside of the U.S. through 2,000 radio outlets. To find a radio station near you, visit **truthforlife.org/stationfinder**.

Free Teaching
The daily program, and Truth For Life's entire teaching library of over 3,000 Bible-teaching messages, can be accessed for free online at **truthforlife.org** and through Truth For Life's mobile app, which can be download for free from your app store.

At-Cost Resources
Books and audio studies from Alistair Begg are available for purchase at cost, with no markup. Visit **truthforlife.org/store**.

Where to Begin?
If you're new to Truth For Life and would like to know where to begin listening and learning, find starting point suggestions at **truthforlife.org/firststep**. For a full list of ways to connect with Truth For Life, visit **truthforlife.org/subscribe**.

Contact Truth For Life
P.O. Box 398000 Cleveland, Ohio 44139
phone 1 (888) 588-7884   **email** letters@truthforlife.org
truthforlife.org

Christian Focus Publications

Our mission statement —

STAYING FAITHFUL

In dependence upon God we seek to impact the world
through literature faithful to His infallible Word, the Bible.
Our aim is to ensure that the Lord Jesus Christ is presented as
the only hope to obtain forgiveness of sin, live a useful life and
look forward to heaven with Him.

Our books are published in four imprints:

CHRISTIAN
FOCUS

Popular works including biographies, commentaries, basic doctrine
and Christian living.

CHRISTIAN
HERITAGE

Books representing some of the
best material from the rich heritage
of the church.

MENTOR

Books written at a level suitable
for Bible College and seminary
students, pastors, and other serious
readers. The imprint includes
commentaries, doctrinal studies,
examination of current issues and
church history.

CF4•K

Children's books for quality Bible
teaching and for all age groups: Sunday
school curriculum, puzzle and activity
books; personal and family devotional
titles, biographies and inspirational stories — because you are never too young
to know Jesus!

Christian Focus Publications Ltd,
Geanies House, Fearn, Ross-shire,
IV20 1TW, Scotland, United Kingdom.
www.christianfocus.com